James Fergusson

The Parthenon; an essay on the mode by which light was introduced into Greek and Roman temples

James Fergusson

The Parthenon; an essay on the mode by which light was introduced into Greek and Roman temples

ISBN/EAN: 9783742875426

Manufactured in Europe, USA, Canada, Australia, Japa

Cover: Foto ©ninafisch / pixelio.de

Manufactured and distributed by brebook publishing software (www.brebook.com)

James Fergusson

The Parthenon; an essay on the mode by which light was introduced into Greek and Roman temples

THE PARTHENON.

LONDON:
PRINTED BY WILLIAM CLOWES AND SONS, LIMITED,
STAMFORD STREET AND CHARING CROSS.

FRONTISPIECE

THE MINERVA OF THE PARTHENON.

THE PARTHENON;

AN ESSAY

ON THE MODE BY WHICH LIGHT WAS INTRODUCED INTO GREEK AND ROMAN TEMPLES.

BY

JAMES FERGUSSON, C.I.E., D.C.L., LL.D.,
F.R.S., F.R.I.B.A., M.R.A.S., Hon. Mem. R.S.L., etc.

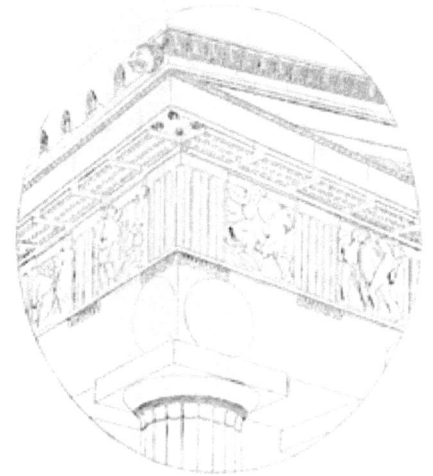

LONDON:
JOHN MURRAY, ALBEMARLE STREET.
1883.

[Right of Translation reserved.]

WORKS BY THE SAME AUTHOR.

ILLUSTRATIONS OF THE ROCK-CUT TEMPLES OF INDIA. 18 Plates in Tinted Lithography, folio; with an 8vo. volume of Texts, Plans, &c. 2l. 7s. 6d. London, Weale, 1845.

PICTURESQUE ILLUSTRATIONS OF ANCIENT ARCHITECTURE IN HINDOSTAN. 24 Plates in Coloured Lithography, with Plans, Woodcuts, and Explanatory Text, &c. &c. London, Hogarth, 1847.

AN HISTORICAL INQUIRY INTO THE TRUE PRINCIPLES OF BEAUTY IN ART, more especially with reference to Architecture. Royal 8vo. 31s. 6d. London, Longmans, 1849.

THE ILLUSTRATED HANDBOOK OF ARCHITECTURE. Being a Concise and Popular Account of the Different Styles prevailing in all Ages and in all Countries. With 850 Illustrations. 8vo. 26s. London, Murray, 1859.

HISTORY OF ARCHITECTURE IN ALL COUNTRIES FROM THE EARLIEST TIMES TO THE PRESENT DAY. In Four Volumes, 8vo., viz.:—
    HISTORY OF ANCIENT AND MEDIÆVAL ARCHITECTURE. Two Vols. 63s. Second Edition. London, Murray, 1874.
    HISTORY OF INDIAN AND EASTERN ARCHITECTURE. One Vol. New Edition. 42s. 1876.
    HISTORY OF THE MODERN STYLES OF ARCHITECTURE. One Vol. 31s. 6d. 1873.

THE PALACES OF NINEVEH AND PERSEPOLIS RESTORED: An Essay on Ancient Assyrian and Persian Architecture. 8vo. 16s. London, Murray, 1851.

THE MAUSOLEUM AT HALICARNASSUS RESTORED IN CONFORMITY WITH THE REMAINS RECENTLY DISCOVERED. Plates. 4to. 7s. 6d. London, Murray, 1862.

RUDE-STONE MONUMENTS IN ALL COUNTRIES, THEIR AGE AND USES. With 234 Illustrations. 8vo. London, Murray, 1872.

TREE AND SERPENT WORSHIP, on ILLUSTRATIONS OF MYTHOLOGY AND ART IN INDIA, in the 1st and 4th Centuries after Christ. 100 Plates and 51 Woodcuts. 4to. London, India Office; and W. H. Allen & Co. 2nd Edition, 1873.

AN ESSAY ON A PROPOSED NEW SYSTEM OF FORTIFICATION, with Hints for its Application to our National Defences. 12s. 6d. London, Weale, 1849.

THE PERIL OF PORTSMOUTH. French Fleets and English Forts. Plans. 8vo. 3s. London, Murray, 1853.

OBSERVATIONS ON THE BRITISH MUSEUM, NATIONAL GALLERY, and NATIONAL RECORD OFFICE; with Suggestions for their Improvement. 8vo. London, Weale, 1850.

AN ESSAY ON THE ANCIENT TOPOGRAPHY OF JERUSALEM; with Restored Plans of the Temple, and with Plans, Sections, and Details of the Church built by Constantine the Great over the Holy Sepulchre, now known as the Mosque of Omar. 4to. Weale, 1847.

THE HOLY SEPULCHRE AND THE TEMPLE AT JERUSALEM. Being the Substance of Two Lectures delivered in the Royal Institution, Albemarle Street, on the 21st February, 1862, and 3rd March, 1865. Woodcuts. 8vo. 7s. 6d. London, Murray, 1865.

THE TEMPLES OF THE JEWS AND THE OTHER BUILDINGS IN THE HARAM AREA AT JERUSALEM. London, Murray, 1878.

PREFACE.

ALTHOUGH so small a portion of this book is devoted directly to the description of the Parthenon, the name of that celebrated temple has been selected to designate the work, for the same reason that Quatremère de Quincy called his essay on Greek Art 'Le Jupiter Olympien.' His work is practically a treatise on Greek sculpture—especially the toreutic branch of it—as then known, and the temple at Elis and the famous chrys-elephantine statue of Phidias occupy relatively a smaller portion of his work than the Parthenon does in mine.

Had the building been entire at the present day, a different mode of treatment from that I have adopted might have been expedient, and it would have been possible to commence with a description of the temple and devote a greater portion of the work to the elucidation of its peculiarities. As it is, the materials out of which it was—in theory—to be reconstructed had to be quarried from various sources, and their forms and uses ascertained, before their application to the Parthenon could be determined. A vast amount of superincumbent rubbish had also to be cleared away before serviceable materials could be got at and gathered together; but once this was done, a few words seemed to be all that was required to explain the application of the forms and ideas gathered from other sources, to the rehabilitation of the lost or misunderstood portions of that famous temple.

So many investigations are now in progress, and so much requires to be done before many of the subjects which are treated of in the following pages can be considered as at all complete, that it is not without considerable reluctance that I publish this work at the present moment. I would not, in fact, hurry it now through the press, but for a feeling that if it is not done now it may possibly not be done at all.

The excavations at Eleusis have actually been commenced at last, but are in so incomplete a state, that I have not been able to obtain even a sketch plan of the results obtained. Those of the Temple of Jupiter Olympius at Athens have not yet been undertaken. I have not been able during the past year to induce any one to open his eyes and observe those features which have an important bearing on the subject of this investigation at Baalbec and Pæstum. M. Rayet's work on his excavations at Didyme in 1873 is still "in the press," and it is uncertain when it may be published; and the details of Mr. Wood's excavations at Ephesus are still buried at the bottom of an old chest at Hammersmith, and we know nothing of them but what can be gleaned from his popular account of his diggings, published 1877.

Some of these deficiencies may no doubt be remedied in a short time, and in some cases the requisite investigations may be hastened by the publication of this work; and if I thought there was any result likely to be obtained from them bearing directly on the line of argument I have adopted, delay might be expedient, at whatever risk. Much will no doubt be added in the next few years to make many of the subjects treated of in these pages more complete; but I am not afraid that anything will be discovered that will invalidate the main argument which they were written to enforce, which, in a few words, may be broadly stated as follows:—

    First. That, as a rule, all Grecian Doric peristylar temples were lighted by opaions or clerestories.

    Second. That Ionic temples, except of the largest class, were generally lighted by windows such as we would use when glass was not available.

    Third. That Corinthian temples were, as a rule, lighted by hypæthra, or pseudo-hypæthra.

    Fourth. That no temple in the ancient world—with the solitary exception of the Pantheon at Rome—was lighted by a horizontal, as contradistinguished from a vertical, opening.

If the demand for the work should prove sufficient to call for a second edition during my lifetime, all the deficiencies arising from imperfect data might be supplied, and errors and mistakes, which inevitably creep in when treating of so novel a subject, could easily be remedied. It is not easy, however, to indulge in illusions in this respect. The work is a strictly special one, on a subject in which very few take any real interest; while it is almost certain to prove offensive to specialists, from the novelty of the views it advocates, and the necessity of expressing them forcibly, in order not to be misunderstood.

The work cannot consequently be expected to be popular, or command an extensive sale; but this is, with me, a very minor consideration. Its elaboration has afforded a pleasant and engrossing occupation during nearly two years, and I am now perfectly content to leave it to those who succeed me in the investigation, as my contribution towards the elucidation of some important points in the history of the most perfect style of architecture with which the world has hitherto been adorned.

CONTENTS.

CHAP.		PAGE
	INTRODUCTION	1
I.—	HYPÆTHRAL TEMPLES	11
II.—	PSEUDO-HYPÆTHRAL TEMPLES	39
III.—	ANCIENT GREEK TEMPLES	52
IV.—	GREEK PERISTYLAR TEMPLES	68
V.—	ABNORMAL GREEK TEMPLES	91
VI.—	THE PARTHENON	105

LIST OF PLATES.

PLATE
    FRONTISPIECE—MINERVA OF THE PARTHENON.
  I.—TEMPLE OF JUPITER OLYMPIUS AT ATHENS
 II.—TEMPLE OF APOLLO EPICURIUS AT BASSÆ
III.—SECTION OF THE PARTHENON ..
IV.—VIEW OF THE INTERIOR OF THE CELLA OF THE PARTHENON

} *At the End.*

LIST OF WOODCUTS.

No.		Page
1.	Remaining Columns and Temple of Jupiter Olympius at Athens	19
2.	Coin of Gordianus, representing the Temple at Miletus	22
3.	Coin representing the Beautiful Gate of the Temple, 131 A.D.	23
4.	Coin of Hadrian	23
5.	Antoninus Pius	23
6.	Pradumenianus	23
7.	Plan of the Cave Temple at Karlé	25
8.	Section of the Chaitya Temple at Karlé	25
9.	View of the Interior of the Chaitya Temple at Karlé	26
10.	Diagram showing the Arrangement of the 127 Columns of the Temple at Ephesus	34
11.	Proposed Restoration of One of the Sculptured Columns at Ephesus	35
12.	Base of Column at Kenawat	36
13.	Section of the Temple of Diana at Nimes	40
14.	Plan of the Temple of Diana at Nimes	40
15.	Prætorium at Moussmieh	41
16.	Section of the Temple of Jupiter at Baalbec	42
17.	Half Section and Half Elevation of the Temple at Baalbec	43
18.	Plan of Temple at Baalbec	43
19.	Doorway at Chaqqa	44
20.	Rock-cut Temple at Cyrene	45
21.	Plan of the Temple of Venus and Rome	46
22.	Half Section of Interior and Half Elevation of Temple of Venus and Rome	47
23.	Diagram Explanatory of suggested Ridge Piece of Temple at Ocra	57
24.	Structure over a Fountain	58
25.	Temple in Antis	58
26.	Angle of the Parthenon	59
27.	Diagram Explanatory of the Mode in which the Primitive Roofs of Greek Temples were formed	64
28.	Diagram of Roof Construction	64
29.	Façade of Tomb at Beni Hassan	65
30.	Ancient Capital from the Southern Temple at Karnac	65
31.	Temple of Themis at Rhamnus	69
32.	Diana Propylæa, Eleusis	69
33.	Temple of Nemesis, Rhamnus	69
34.	Temple of Artemis, Orchygia	71
35.	Section of Temple at Ægina	72
36.	Plan of Temple at Ægina	72
37.	Temple of Apollo Epicurius at Bassæ	75
38.	Roof of Temple at Bassæ, showing the Opaion	76
39.	One of the Perforated Tiles	76
40.	Isometric View of Opening in Roof, Bassæ	77
41.	Section of the Temple of Neptune at Pæstum	82
42.	Plan of Temple of Neptune at Pæstum	82
43.	Capital of Upper Order, Pæstum	83
44.	Restored Section of the Heræon, Olympia	87
45.	Plan and Section of the Hyræon, Olympia	87
46.	Plan of the Great Temple at Agrigentum	94
47.	Section of Roof of Great Temple at Agrigentum	95
48.	Elevation of Upper Part of Cella Walls, Agrigentum	95
49.	Great Temple at Selinus	94
50.	Section of Central Portion of Great Hall at Karnac	98
51.	Plan of Hypostyle Hall at Karnac	98
52.	Restored Section of the Temple at Eleusis	99
53.	Plan of the Temple at Eleusis	99
54.	Plan of Parthenon in its present state, but showing the Remains of the Christian Church	105
55.	Diagram of suggested Rearrangement of the Interior of the Parthenon	108
56.	Church of Sta. Agnese, Rome	113
57.	San Lorenzo Fuori le Mura, Rome	114
58.	Ornament in Imitation of Bronze from a Capital of the Temple of the Smintheian Apollo	115
59.	Diagram showing the Plan and Elevation of the Opening of the Roof of the Parthenon	118
60.	Angle of Roof of Parthenon	119

THE PARTHENON.

INTRODUCTION.

AMONG all the various architectural problems which antiquity has left for our solution none seems so difficult, though at the same time so interesting, as that which aims at explaining how light was introduced into the interior of classical temples. Hitherto no satisfactory explanation has been offered, or was indeed to be expected, partly because at the time the temples were erected the mode in which it was done was so usual and universally known, that no author has thought it worth while to leave a description of it; partly because if introduced through the roof—which is the theory now generally adopted—all those, which were principally in wood, have perished, and left no trace of their original form of construction. But more, perhaps, owing to the strange atrophy into which true architectural art has fallen, from a false system of blind copying without thought, which is the characteristic of its state at the present day. Had men from the beginning of the controversy thought only of how light could best be introduced, they would soon have found out how it was done by the Greeks, and the verbal and constructive puzzles would soon have been swept away and forgotten. As it is, more has been written and more angry controversies have arisen regarding this than with reference to any other feature, either constructive or artistic, in the temples of the ancients, and none ought apparently ever to have arisen had only a little common sense been applied to the solution of the problem from the beginning.

When, in 1815, Quatremère de Quincy published his famous essay on the Olympian Jupiter, he wrote: "Il règne une assez parfaite unanimité, entre tous les écrivains modernes, sur l'opinion que les temples des anciens, ou ne recevaient pas de lumière, ou n'en recevaient que par l'ouverture de leur porte;" and he quotes in support of this opinion the names of Spon and Wheeler, Perrault, Gagliani, Simon, l'Abbé Barthélemy, le Baron Riedesel, Winckelmann, Chandler, Stieglitz, Silenkeez, Rossa, d'Argenville, and many others.[1]

From this enumeration he omits our countryman Stuart, to whom, however, he does ample justice in an essay written apparently in 1805, though not

---

[1] Le Jupiter Olympien, p. 262.

published before 1826,[1] in which he discusses his views on the subject at considerable length. Unfortunately Stuart drew no diagram, nor did he leave any separate essay on the subject, but from what he says[2] we are justified in inferring that he was, if not the first, at least among the first to propose lighting the temples by partially removing the roof. To what extent he would have done this is not quite clear, but the principle was then announced which has since been very generally adopted.

Whoever was the first to suggest this theory, Quatremère was the first to give it form and significance in the plates of his 'Jupiter Olympien.' There the opening is figured in the form and in the position which he considers requisite for the proper illumination of the statue, and he thus placed the controversy on a new and distinct basis. In all succeeding controversies it was contended either that the temples were illuminated by this opening in the roof—a skylight in fact—or the authors reverted to the old contention that no light was admitted except through the doors, or by artificial means. In this essay he takes immense, and as it seems in the present day unnecessary pains, to prove that it was not by lamplight that the temples were lighted. No one who considers for a moment how imperfect the means at the disposal of the Greeks were in this respect, would perhaps put forward such a suggestion. Even if it were considered possible to accumulate a sufficient number of lamps to effect a proper illumination, the contingency, on the opening of a door, of having them all blown out would be sufficient to prevent their adoption. Without glass shades this would inevitably occur, and the smoke and smell be too horrid to contemplate.[3]

Unfortunately for the acceptance of his views on this subject, Quatremère restored the temple at Olympia with a semicircular, or rather semi-elliptical vault in wood, of singularly weak form and design. It was felt that this vault was so repugnant to all we knew of Greek architecture that though critics could not quite say why it should not have been adopted, they felt that it was impossible, and generally passed it by in silence. He was induced to adopt this form of roof principally from an expression in Strabo, who, when describing the seated statue of Jupiter that adorned this temple, says it was so colossal that it nearly touched the summit of the roof (τῇ κορυφῇ τῆς ὀροφῆς); and that if it stood upright it would carry away the roof altogether.[4] From this he argued that the expression could not apply to a flat ceiling, which could have no summit, while on the other hand a vault had, and to this only was the expression applicable. He was further

---

[1] Mémoire sur la manière dont étaient éclairés les Temples des Grecs et Romains. Memoires de l'Institut Hist. et Lit. Anc. tome iii. p. 242, 1818.

[2] Antiquities of Athens, 1787, vol. ii. pp. 7 and 10.

[3] No one in Europe now thinks of advocating this mode of lighting Greek temples, but an American has recently brought it forward. Across the water they seem to have to go through all the stages of the controversy till they arrive where we now are. It is only to be hoped, as in most things, the stages will be infinitely more rapid than with us. [4] Strabo, 353.

confirmed in this view by finding a number of coins representing apparently the interior of temples (sections in fact) with arched forms over the statues.[1] In this also he probably was correct, but he was unable to adduce anything to connect these representations, which are generally late Roman, with the temple at Olympia. The result was that though his views are expressed with great diffidence and moderation, they failed to carry conviction to the minds of inquirers.

The only architect of eminence who subsequently has adopted De Quincy's proposal of a circular roof to Greek temples is Edward Falkener. In his 'Dædalus'[2] he adopted a semicircular roof for the Parthenon, employing in its defence the same arguments that were used by De Quincy, but adopting them mainly because, except by means of a vault, he fancied he could not find room for the colossal height of the statue of Minerva as described by Pliny.[3] This however is a difficulty entirely of his own raising. He assumes that the 26 cubits of Pliny apply only to the statue of the goddess, exclusive of the pedestal on which she stands, while the description, taken as a whole, seems to imply that Pliny included the pedestal with its sculptures as part of the group, and that his measurement of height was taken from the floor line. But even if this were not so there are other means, without resorting to the extreme expedient of vaulting, by which the statue, with a moderate pedestal, could be accommodated under a properly designed roof. But of this hereafter. Meanwhile it is curious to observe how much our knowledge of the details of Greek architecture has progressed during the half-century that has elapsed between the publication of these two works. Instead of the weak mean vault of De Quincy we have one of great architectural beauty and strength; but this only serves to bring out more forcibly the defects of the system. To leave an opening in the eye of a dome is mechanically correct. It relieves the vault of weight, where weight is injurious to stability, and, with a circular rim round it, its form is constructively correct in every respect. But on the other hand to cut a square opening in a waggon vault —to remove the keystone in fact—is an architectural solecism which we may feel sure the sense of architectural propriety in a Greek would never have tolerated in any vault, either in stone or wood. Besides this, the wandering light from a naked skylight would have been most inartistic and disagreeable; not only because of the glaring sun that must have shone on the worshippers at mid-day, but of the rain and snow against which, on this system, it was impossible to provide any protection. Everything, in fact, combined to render this mode of lighting the temple most objectionable, while the gain in height was insignificant. In the section, Plate III. of this work, the thickness from the summit outside to the under side of the beam is 7 feet. In Mr. Falkener's section (page 18) it is 5 feet, with difficulties of construction which seem almost insuperable.

---

[1] Quatremère de Quincy, loc. cit.
[2] Dædalus, or the causes and principles of the excellence of Greek Sculpture. Longman and Co. 1860.
[3] Pliny, l. xxxvi. c. v.

A better scheme to meet the same supposed difficulty in the Parthenon was suggested by Canina in 1841.[1] He proposed to raise the external roof so as to form a baldacchino over the statue in such a manner as to protect it from the direct influence of the weather. If he had had the courage to carry this raised roof forward to the eastern end of the cella, it would have been a solution of the difficulty in so far as the Parthenon was concerned. A not very probable one, it must be confessed, and not applicable to other temples, nor easily defended by argument, but still mechanically correct. Unfortunately in front of the statue he left the whole of the cella uncovered by any roof, and so induced all the inconveniences and anomalies inherent in all schemes for removing either a portion or the whole of the roofs of these temples.

While these restorations were being offered as solutions of the difficulty, the abstract question was argued with great vehemence and immense learning both in Germany and France. In the former country Dr. Ludwig Ross opened the ball with vigour in his 'Hellenica'[2] in an article entitled 'Keine Hypæthral Tempel mehr,' and proved his contention entirely to his own satisfaction, and to that probably of many others, with an amount of learning which is really appalling. He was answered with equal and even greater learning by C. Boetticher[3] in a powerful pamphlet he wrote on the subject, in which he certainly seems to have the best of the argument; and any impartial judge would probably assign to him the palm of victory, had he not vitiated his cause by one of the most singular *non sequiturs* that probably ever occurred in this or any other controversy. In the course of his researches, he discovered in the Digests of the Roman law, compiled during the reign of Justinian, that it was a disputed point among the lawyers, whether the "Stratura, ex tabulis factis, quæ æstate tollerentur, et hieme ponerentur" were tenants' fixtures, or belonged to the freehold.[4] This "Stratura" was avowedly a temporary expedient adopted in private houses, to close the openings or hatchways that led to the flat roofs of the houses, and which naturally were closed when no longer used, as they would be in winter. It is hardly to be supposed that they covered any part of the court-yard, or places of ordinary resort. On the contrary, these would require in winter all the warmth and light of the sun more than in summer, and anything that would obscure and interrupt this would be especially objectionable.

Be this as it may, it certainly was a most extraordinary conclusion to arrive at, that because this temporary expedient was adopted in private houses five or six centuries after Christ, it was adopted by the Greeks in their most monumental buildings six centuries before that epoch. Yet M. Boetticher so restores

---

[1] Canina, Architectura Greca, fol. Roma, 1831-41, pls. lvii. lviii.
[2] Hellenica, 1 Band, 1 Heft, Halle, 1846.
[3] Der Hypæthraltempel auf grund des Vitruvischen Zeugnisses gegen Professor L. Ross Berlin, Ernst und Korn (no date).
[4] Digest, 446. 242. § 2.

the Temple of Neptune at Pæstum. He covers the whole area of the cella and even the peristyles with a flat ceiling apparently in plaster, and protects this with a roof of planks like a booth in a fair. He does this on the assumption that for four or six months during the winter the temples were deserted and left in darkness, and that only in summer the planks were removed and the religious ceremonies of the people resumed. In proposing this he forgets that during the summer thunderstorms of unusual suddenness and violence occur in these regions, and that one such would not only bring down its flat ceiling, but flood the whole temple and destroy everything in it long before the planking could be replaced to protect it.[1] It certainly was not thus that the Greeks roofed their temples. The fact, however, that this mode of roofing should have been proposed by a scholar of such learning, and so beautiful a draftsman as Boetticher certainly is, and who had paid such attention to the subject, is sufficient to show how little the *litera scripta* bearing on the subject is capable of explaining the difficulty, and how hopeless it is to seek a solution in this direction.

In France Letronne and Raoul Rochette enacted the same parts as had been played by Ross and Boetticher in Germany—the former contending with great force of reasoning that no light was admitted to Greek temples, except through the doorway;[2] the latter, with equal logic, proving that the principal source of light was an opening of greater or less extent in the roof,[3] a view which has been more generally adopted by subsequent enquirers. But perhaps one of the most striking, as it is one of the most obvious proofs, how idle these controversies are, is to be found in two restorations of temples which recently have appeared in France. In 1877 the 'Ecole des Beaux Arts' published a large volume adorned with twenty-one folio plates, purporting to be a restoration of the temples at Pæstum, by Labrouste. Among them the celebrated Temple of Neptune is represented with a solid roof without any opening whatever—the cella, 90 feet in depth and raised 6 feet above the floor of the peristyles, and represented as perfectly illuminated, though the only light that could penetrate to it was admitted through the doorway, 12 or 13 feet wide, placed behind a double range of columns at a distance of 50 feet from the open air.[4] The cella of a temple so arranged must have been in nearly total darkness during even the brightest of days, and the statue of the god, which was placed at its inner

---

[1] I long thought I must have mistaken Boetticher's meaning, and misunderstood a section of the temple at Pæstum (Tektonik der Hellenen, pl. 25, v. ii. pp. 364 and 325,) but I find that Hittorff (Architecture Antique de la Sicile, p. 297) takes the same view, though its absurdity does not seem to have struck him to the extent it has me.

[2] Journal des Savants, Nov. Dec. 1846 and Feb. 1847.

[3] Revue Archéologique, 1848.

[4] It is much to be regretted that works of this sort, published at the expense of Government, should be sold at prices which are absolutely prohibitory to students. 150 francs for 21 plates, with a very scant text, is twice as much as any publisher in this country would dare to ask for such a work. Do they manage these things so much better in France?

extremity, 150 feet from the light, must have been absolutely invisible. The other restoration is that of the smaller so-called Temple of Jupiter at Egina, published by Charles Garnier, in the 'Revue Archéologique' for 1854, pp. 193 and 345. In this, the author, who seems to have studied the subject with infinite care, proposes to roof solidly the open porticos both of the pronaos and posticum, but removes the roof entirely from the cella. In it the statue of Jupiter, in wood and ivory apparently, is left sitting literally in the open air without any protection whatever against the weather, though snow must have fallen on him in winter, and torrents of rain at some seasons of the year. The dark cell in which his brother Neptune was confined at Pæstum was certainly a preferable abode to this; but the curious thing is that neither of these authors seems to be aware of the absurdity of the libel they are uttering against the Greeks. Generally it is supposed—and justly so—that they were not only the most artistic but the most ingenious people that ever existed. Their temples are subjects of unceasing admiration to those who properly understand them. Their statues were the most elaborate and most beautiful the world has yet seen, and the ornaments of the temples the richest and the most varied that could be conceived. Yet with all this it is assumed that they could not put such a roof on their temples as would protect them from the weather and introduce sufficient light either through the walls or the roof to light the interior in a sufficient and satisfactory manner. No other people in any part of the world have found any difficulty in effecting this, and it seems a monstrous proposition to assume that the Greeks alone failed to accomplish it. It would be better to confess at once that we did not know anything about the matter, and had no suggestion to make, than perpetrate such libels as are involved in such attempts at restoration as these.

Among recent writers on the subject there is perhaps no one who has approached the subject in a greater spirit of fairness, or treated it more philosophically than Hittorff. His 'Architecture Antique de la Sicile,' published in 1870, is a worthy successor to Quatremère de Quincy's 'Jupiter Olympien,' and supplements it with all the additional information acquired by the researches of the succeeding half-century. In a work ranging over such a wide field of history and of art, it is impossible to agree with many of the conclusions he arrives at; but even these may always be read with profit for the suggestions they afford.

In the course of his work he naturally devotes a considerable space to the mode in which Greek temples were lighted, but does not seem to have arrived at any very definite conclusion regarding it. Generally he, like most architects, favours the idea that it was by a simple opening in the ridge of the roof, and he so restores the Temple R at Selinus—the only one of the Selinuntine temples which he thinks it necessary to provide with any means of lighting except by the doorway, though to ordinary observers—looking on the plan—

others required it more than this one. In the plate (87) on which he describes the mode in which he conceives light was introduced into the Parthenon, he evidently inclines to the same system,[1] though this involves stretching the double columns of the interior to a height of upwards of 50 feet, while recent researches show that not more than 40 were admissible.[2] As if, however, he was not quite confident that this was the mode of lighting adopted in the Parthenon, he suggested another (Plate 87, fig. F. vii.), which seems hardly to be an improvement upon it. According to this scheme two openings are made on each side of the ridge, about 25 feet in length, and about one third of that in breadth,[3] through which the light was admitted. The defect of this system is, the rain, instead of falling on the floor of the temple, falls on to that of the gallery, where it is much more objectionable. It probably also was introduced in great quantities, for it would be difficult to divert that falling on the ridge and on each side of it. But the greatest defect is that light is introduced only through the interstices of the upper range of columns in a most inartistic manner below the head of the statue and leaving the roof in comparative darkness.

Neither of these systems seems to have satisfied him entirely, because when he restored the great temple at Selinus (Temple T) he adopted with the slightest possible modification, though with very scant acknowledgment (p. 497), the system I had proposed twenty years before, the untenableness of which he had just been busy in exposing. How little he understood its principles may be gathered from the fact of his applying it in a manner I never would have dreamt of doing, and to a temple which certainly was roofed by some other system. Practically, every drop of rain that fell over the immense cella of the temple fell into it, and no means were applied for its discharge.

The only other author of any eminence that in recent times has written on the subject is M. Charles Chipiez. In an article in the 'Revue Archéologique' for April 1878 he proposes a system of lighting, which is practically the same as the second suggestion of M. Hittorff, though without some of its merits. In some very beautiful and elaborate drawings[4] he shows how he would propose to apply it to the so-called Temple of Jupiter in Egina. Externally he does this in a manner which is unobjectionable in appearance, but internally has the same objection as was pointed out in speaking of M. Hittorff's, that all the rain that fell over the lateral openings fell on the gallery floors internally (it is more than doubtful if there were any galleries at Egina), and then must either have dropped on the floor or have been allowed to evaporate. Besides this, it is very doubtful whether a perfectly flat cymatium more than 40 feet

---

[1] Loc. cit. pl. 87. fig. F. v. P. vii. p. 294.
[2] See further on sections of Temples at Egina and Pestum.
[3] The plan is so small, and both the references to it and the scale are wrong, so it is difficult to quote exactly.
[4] The drawings, though done with all the skill and art of the French in perspective drawing, are very unintelligible. One simple honest section would have told the story far more clearly.

in length could be constructed in marble so as to be water-tight, and throw off the storm rains as he proposed. If it could not, the whole of the rain that fell on either side of the ridge must have fallen into the opening. Even with metal gutters it would have been most difficult to prevent this, and certainly metal was not used for that purpose. The great defect, as pointed out before, is not constructive but artistic. The light is introduced too low between the pillars of the upper range of columns below the head of the statue, and leaving the roof in comparative gloom.

Were anything to be gained by it, it would be easy to extend these remarks on bygone attempts to solve the problem to any required length. Enough has, however, probably been said to explain how they failed, and from what causes. There is one instance, however, still remaining which is worth while noticing as a most curious example of the modern system of practising architecture. Among English architects there probably was no more enlightened scholar or more elegant artist than the late Professor Cockerell. When he published his beautiful work on the 'Temples at Egina and Bassæ,'[1] he had evidently opportunities of solving the question which have fallen to the lot of no one else—these temples being the two which retain more of their original arrangement than any others in Greece. So strange, however, is this system of modern art, that he never seems to have thought twice about it. He found in the cella of the temple at Egina two rows of columns, with others standing on the heads, with only a useless architrave between them. They were not wanted to support galleries, because there were none, nor to support the roof, for the cella was only 24 feet wide, and the Greeks roofed far wider spaces both at Athens and Olympia. It was a weak and ugly form, which even the exquisite art of the Greeks could never render tolerable. Why then was it introduced? Modern architects don't think, and it never occurred even to the learned Professor to ask himself this question. He had learned that the mode of lighting was by a hole in the roof, and he never thought of enquiring whether this strange and elaborate apparatus might be connected with the mode in which light was introduced. In like manner when he described and drew the temple at Bassæ with such elaboration and detail, the same phenomenon occurred without exciting his attention. In this instance there was a considerable advance in design on the former example. Instead of two stories of Doric columns, one taller Ionic order eked out with a frieze and cornice sufficed nearly to reach the roof. Instead of being supported by single buttress-stones as at Egina, these were attached to the wall throughout the whole height; but to the casual observer they were used for some apparently useless purpose—either it was to narrow the cella, only 22 feet wide, or to strengthen the walls, which already were of sufficient

[1] The Temples of Jupiter Panhellenius at Egina and Apollo Epicurius at Bassæ, by C. R. Cockerell, London, Weale, 1860.

thickness to support all they had to carry. The plan, too, presented anomalies most difficult to account for. The pillars next the door were jammed up against it in a most clumsy manner. Those at the further end of the cella were thrust forward diagonally in a manner equally inexplicable. In fact, there is not among all the Greek temples known so clumsy a piece of planning as this, unless there were a motive for its eccentricities. But the difference between a true and copying art is this, that the Greeks placed no stone and no moulding where it had not an obvious object and meaning, which can be easily detected by those who really seek to understand the language in which it is expressed. A modern architect on the contrary employs these forms merely as ornaments without the least reference to the purpose for which they were invented or the uses to which they were originally devoted. When Mr. Cockerell built the Taylor and Randolph Institute at Oxford he used the Ionic columns he had learned to admire at Bassae, but merely as ornaments, combined with features which rendered their employment not only—as pillars—useless and even hurtful to the design, and where even his exquisite taste and feeling could not prevent their appearing ridiculous. It is indeed this false system of art that lies at the root of all our perplexities on this question. If, instead of puzzling themselves with obscure or corrupt texts and false analogies, architects had set to work to discover, from existing remains, how Greek temples could best be lighted, the question would long ago have been solved. The Greeks were neither fools nor savages, but on the contrary the cleverest architects we know or knew of, and we have every reason to believe that the interiors of the temples were as perfect as we know the exteriors to have been. To contend, therefore, that they alone of all the people in the world could not put a weather-tight roof on the temples, while admitting the requisite quantity of light for their illumination, seems one of the most monstrous propositions that ever was put forward. There are many ways in which the end might be accomplished without much taxing their ingenuity. One of the most obvious was to introduce a range of openings high up the cella walls under the peristyles. Windows so situated would have been perfectly protected from the weather in all circumstances, and the light introduced so situated as, according to our ideas, to meet all the artistic exigencies of the case. If it was not adopted—as we know it never was—it must have been that the Greek architects knew of some better expedient, which was mechanically as perfect, and artistically was better, and this they adopted in preference to what appears to us the most obviously practical mode of introducing light. What that was, it is the object of this treatise to explain.

In the meanwhile if at an earlier stage of the investigation, any one with even the most moderate appreciation of the talents and position of the Greek architects could have shown that there was a better mode of lighting their temples than by the doorway, it ought unhesitatingly to have been adopted as more likely to have been used by the Greeks; or if any one could have invented any better

c

mode than the hole in the roof, that for the same reason ought to have been preferred, or, in short, the more nearly we could approach perfection the more nearly we probably should reach a knowledge of the mode adopted in Grecian temples. This, however, is not the mode of investigation adopted by any who have hitherto attempted the solution of the problem; hence the immense amount of ink spilt in discussions which have no real bearing on the subject, and could not possibly lead to any satisfactory conclusion.

When in 1848 I was collecting information for my work on 'The True Principles of Beauty in Art,' I, as a matter of course, read all the works then within my reach on this subject, and very soon became convinced that the "litera scripta" did not furnish the materials requisite for a solution of the problems connected with the mode in which classical temples were lighted. I consequently determined to try and find out whether any other mode of investigation was likely to lead to more satisfactory results. For this purpose I examined carefully the plans of all the Greek temples then available, and drew sections and restorations of them, in so far as their ruined state then admitted of this being done. I had not proceeded far in this line of research before I arrived at the prosaic, but common-sense conclusion, that the Greeks, like every other people, in every part of the world, introduced light into their buildings by vertical openings; or, in other words, by windows—in the case of temples generally countersunk in the roofs, though sometimes also placed in the walls; in all other public and private buildings vertical openings were also the only mode adopted. In fact that they did what all people must have done before the invention of glass, which alone rendered horizontal openings practicable, without exposing them to all the vicissitudes of atmospheric disturbance.

These results I embodied in my 'True Principles of Beauty in Art,' in a section especially devoted to the "Hypæthron" (pp. 385-393), illustrated by six woodcuts and one plate. For the latter I chose the temple at Bassæ as an "instantia crucis," being one of the most difficult, but at the same time the one which affords the most obvious means of illustrating the system. I did not then think it necessary to go more into detail—enough I thought was said to make it clear, to any one who cared about the matter, what was meant, and how it could be applied to all temples. Once the principle was announced, it appeared to me then, that it would be generally adopted as a solution of the difficulty without opposition. The result, as is well known, was widely different. The theory was treated with contempt, and so far as I can recollect, was not noticed by any critic or by any author at the time. Every one is aware of the proverbial difficulty of making a horse drink if not so inclined. The public would have none of my theories, and there was nothing for it but to submit. I thought no more of the matter till, twelve years afterwards, Ed. Falkener, moved to wrath by some anonymous criticism on his 'Dædalus,' wrote a pamphlet in answer, and availed himself of the opportunity, which he had long sought, of saying a few words in disparagement of my theories regarding the hypæthron, which were diametrically opposed to those he had enunciated.[1]

This gave me an opportunity of bringing the subject before the Royal Institute of British Architects, which I did in a paper I read to them in November 1861,[2] which excited considerable attention at the time, and was followed by a discussion, in which several of the leading architects and some distinguished amateurs took part. The result was very much what I should, from subsequent experience, have been led to expect. No one frankly adopted my views. Every one had some objection, more or less relevant, to offer; but except Mr. Ashpitel, who on that occasion acted as the mouthpiece of Mr. Falkener, no one had studied the question to the extent necessary to form a competent opinion on the subject. In one sense the discussion was eminently satisfactory to me. Though all were hostile not one had hit on any flaw in the argument, or pointed out any difficulty in carrying out my views, and no one ventured then to assert that the mode of lighting which I had suggested was not adapted to the purposes for which it was intended.

This being so, I felt perfectly content, in my own mind, that my views must ultimately prevail—not probably in my lifetime—and thought no more of the matter, and probably never should, but that twenty-one years after this discussion I undertook to write an introduction to the fourth volume of the 'Antiquities of Ionia' for the Dilettanti Society. To do this satisfactorily, in order to express an opinion on such points as had not been cleared up, I found it necessary to go again over the whole subject of the architecture of Greek temples, and their arrangements. Of these, however, I did not consider the mode of lighting as one requiring reiteration on the present occasion, and consequently on page 8 merely inserted a paragraph describing the mode of lighting I had proposed thirty-three years before. While the work was in the press, and before it had been printed off, Mr. Newton sent me a copy of the 'Oeffentlicher Anzeiger,' which contained an official report from Herr Dörpfeld, one of the architects engaged in the excavations at Olympia undertaken by the German Government. It was dated from Olympia, in January 1881, and was countersigned by Dr. F. Adler, the chief of the exploring staff in Berlin, 8th of February. In this Herr Dörpfeld states unhesitatingly "that they had found the hypæthron of the Greek temple there, and also the impluvium, in a manner that leaves no doubt that the light was introduced in the manner usually suggested."[3] On reading the passage

---

[1] On the Hypæthron of Greek Temples, together with some observations in reply to the Reviewers of Didymus, Longman, 1861.

[2] Published in their Sessional Papers for 1861–62.

[3] "Unmittelbar vor dem Bilde befand sich genau in der Mitte des Tempels ein vertiefter, von weissem Marmor umgebener, ca. 6·50 m. breiter Fussboden aus schwarzem Kalkstein = der Platz unter dem Hypæthron. Hier stand unter freiem Himmel der von Pausanias erwähnte Opferaltar und die eherne Urne,

carefully over it appeared to me so evident that what the Germans had found was merely the arrangement described in such detail by Pausanias[1] for supplying the statue with oil, that had I been writing my own book I should not have noticed this fancied discovery. But as I was only one of a sub-committee publishing a work in the name of the Dilettanti Society, and supposed consequently to be expressing the opinion of the members, who might be considered as responsible for what was published in their name, I cancelled the paragraph. In its place I substituted a very indefinite one which may be read either as expressing belief in Herr Dörpfeld's views of the matter or my own.

This incident, though trivial in itself, determined me at once to go on with a model of the Parthenon, which I long had contemplated making, but never carried into effect. It was not important for the purpose of convincing myself of the correctness of my views, and probably would be useless in convincing those that were opposed to them, but there were certain things which it was difficult to ascertain or be sure about without trying them experimentally in a model. As it is, I have no reason to regret having made it. In the first place it has enabled me to ascertain, within very narrow limits, the extent of the openings in the roof, which are required for lighting the statue properly, and also their position, which without the assistance of the model would be difficult. The form of the roof, too, though it might have been thought out by itself, was suggested by seeing how unpleasant a flat ceiling was as usually adopted, and various other details were either suggested or their employment confirmed by the experience thus gained.

Under these circumstances it appears to me that the subject has passed beyond the limits of controversy. A mode of lighting Greek temples has been elaborated which answers all the required conditions of the problem, as at present known to us, and which, so far as we can form an opinion, is nearly perfect. While this is so, it seems absurd to go on splitting hairs, or indulging in verbal controversies in defence of systems which are avowedly imperfect. Still, men must be allowed to go on quoting Vitruvius as saying "sub divo, sine tecto," without any reference to the context, or without attaching any distinct meaning to the words used, and repeat the usual formula of dissent or disparagement because they have been in the habit of so doing. All these, and other "fatal objections" will, no doubt, continue to be urged, for it would never do to allow any one credit for doing anything they have not themselves suggested. But all this will die out in time in the face of truth, and, if I am right, the views explained in this work will pass from the region of controversy to those of accepted facts. But if this mode of criticism is closed, another, and far more profitable one, is open, and

welche nach der Lokalsage die Stelle bezeichnete, die Zeus mit seinem Blitz getroffen hatte. Die Marmorziegel, welche die hierüber befindliche Öffnung im Dache einfassten, sind gefunden, und auch die bautechnische Anlage, durch welche das einfallende Regenwasser und das von dem Bilde herabläufende Öl abgeleitet wurden, ist entdeckt worden."

[1] Pausanias, vol. ii. p. 183.

may afford an opportunity for a vast amount of ingenuity. It is to improve on what I have suggested. I am very far from fancying I have exhausted the subject. There may be many points I have missed, some I have misunderstood, and to these attention might be profitably directed. I am not afraid that the foundation of my system will be undermined, but I have no doubt the superstructure may be improved; to this then I earnestly invite co-operation.

Meanwhile, I believe that the system of lighting here proposed may at least claim the merit of being mechanically perfect, and in accordance with all the architectural features of all the buildings known to exist. Artistically it renders the interior of the building as beautiful as the exterior, and that is saying a great deal, and is a more perfect mode of lighting statues than has since been seen or practised anywhere in modern times. Historically every feature can be traced back to its origin, and throughout there is not, so far as I know, anywhere one word or assertion that contradicts it in any way. If this is so, as I trust it will appear in these pages, the system may, it appears to me, be accepted as a fact, till at least some better is invented to take its place.

In so far as I am able to form an opinion, there is one infallible test by which we may judge of the truth or falsehood of any theory of Greek architectural art. We must never for one instant lose sight of the acknowledged fact that the Greeks were in their great age the most ingenious and the most artistic people the world ever knew. When, therefore, the result of our enquiries leads us to any form less perfect, either mechanically or artistically, than we would adopt at the present day, we may feel sure that there is some flaw in the argument, that we are on a wrong path, and that the conclusion may safely be rejected. If, on the contrary, our investigations lead up to anything as perfect, or more so than was ever done elsewhere, in the same circumstances and with the same materials, we may be pretty sure it was very nearly the mode that was adopted by the Greeks. Nothing that we inartistic Anglo-Saxons can ever imagine will nearly realize the perfection of the glories of the Parthenon as designed by Ictinus and adorned by Phidias; but I conceive I have gone further in this direction than has hitherto been done, either from a constructive or an artistic point of view. With a larger model and more thought I might go still nearer, but this I may confidently leave to others, being content to have pointed out the path by which the glories of Greek art are to be approached.

CHAPTER I.

HYPÆTHRAL TEMPLES.

It may not appear a very logical mode of proceeding to describe the manner in which light was introduced into Roman temples before attempting to grapple with the problem of lighting those of Greece, which it is the principal object of this treatise to explain. If the subject were in so advanced a state as to be treated historically this mode of proceeding would, of course, be absurd; but as it now stands a vast amount of rubbish requires to be cleared away, and many misunderstandings corrected, before an historical treatment is possible. In the present instance it will consequently be convenient, if not logical, to reverse the ordinary mode of treatment, otherwise it would be almost impossible to obtain a hearing for what has to be said with regard to the earlier Greek temples. Fortunately no inconvenience is likely to arise in this instance from the abandonment of the historical sequence. The mode of lighting temples invented by the Greeks was not, apparently, adopted in any single instance by the Roman architects. Their mode of introducing the necessary illumination was, so far as it can be made out, a modification of the hypæthral arrangement of a class of exceptional temples of the Greeks, and applied by them in a perfectly original manner, easily distinguished from that of their Grecian predecessors.

The truth of the matter seems to be, that nearly all the confusion that still hangs about the subject arises mainly from authors not taking the trouble to classify the subject, and applying to early and late temples indiscriminately, any assertion that may be found as applying either to the early Greek or late Roman examples. It would be quite as reasonable to argue regarding the form of mediæval Catholic churches from the forms of those built during the reign of Queen Anne. They were both Christian, and we are now told used for a ritual practically identical, in outward forms at least. But the square-galleried halls, with two stories of round-headed sash windows, are very different from the long-drawn aisles and mullioned clerestories of Gothic churches. But if we had only books and descriptions to depend upon, they might be considered as identical, and it would be extremely difficult from any "litera scripta" to point out the distinction between the two. Certainly Sir Christopher Wren and his contemporaries did not see any essential difference. If, however, we would understand the subject we must carefully discriminate between them, and be most careful not to apply to the one what only belongs to the other. The history of the two styles, if properly examined, ought to have sufficed to warn authors of the extreme probability of the existence of such a difference. There was, in fact, no Grecian Doric temple of any importance built after the age of Alexander the Great (325 B.C.). No Roman Corinthian temple, that we know of, was erected before the time of Pompey (75 B.C.), unless, indeed, the Temple of Jupiter Olympius at Athens is to be considered as a Roman temple, as it was designed by a Roman architect,[1] in the second century before the Christian era. The two centuries and a half that elapsed between the two epochs is nearly a blank in architectural history, imperfectly bridged over by a few Ionic temples in Asia Minor, which have only the slightest possible connexion with the Grecian Doric that preceded them, or the Roman Corinthian that succeeded them. So much, indeed, is this the case, that, for the present at least, they may be safely put on one side, while we may at our option take up either the subject of the Corinthian or the Doric, as they are separated from each other by so long a period of time. They belong in reality to a different people, and were used for religions differing from each other as much at least as Roman Catholic does from Anglican Protestant forms.

When, however, we restrict our researches to Roman architecture only, we are not much further advanced than we were. It is true that we have the great work of Vitruvius, in ten books, devoted wholly to architecture, the only work of the sort that has reached us. In it he professes to tell us all that is known regarding not only temples, but public and private buildings; and, had he been a more methodical author, he ought to have left nothing of an important architectural character uncertain or undescribed. The contrary, however, may be said to be nearly always the case. He has added, indeed, very little to the knowledge we derive from the buildings themselves, and scarcely one of his statements can be accepted without verification. With regard to the lighting of temples, there is only one paragraph bearing directly upon it, and that is unfortunately so corrupt that it is impossible to rely upon it. This, however, is not Vitruvius's fault, but it is our misfortune, and arises from the doctoring his text has been subjected to by early editors. It has been avowedly tampered with, though no one knows by whom, and in consequence has given rise to almost all the misunderstandings that have arisen on the subject.

The passage in question, forming the second chapter of the third book, though too long to quote, requires to be read *in extenso* in order to understand its whole bearing on the question at issue. He first describes temples in antis, then those which are prostyle and amphiprostyle. He then proceeds to describe hexastyle peripteral temples, of which he quotes several examples, but without one word as to the mode in which they were lighted. The next class of temples he mentions are the pseudodipteral. They had eight pillars in the front and in the posticum, but the walls of the cella range with the central four, so that a space of two

---

[1] Vitruvius, lib. vii. præf.

columns is left in the ambulatory. He then goes on to say: "The dipteros is octastyle in the pronaos and posticum, but round the cella has a double order of columns, as in the Doric temple of Quirinus at Rome, and the Ionic temple of Diana at Ephesus, built by Chersiphrones." After this comes the important passage, which is the only one bearing on the question before us: "Hypæthral temples are, indeed, decastyle in the pronaos and posticum; in every other respect they are the same as the dipteral (temples), but in the interior they have double columns in two heights, remote from the walls, to admit of circulation in the same manner as the porticoes of the peristyle. The middle, however, is open to the air—under heaven—and without a roof. They are approached by doors at both ends in the pronaos and posticum. There is no example of this kind of temple at Rome, but at Athens," as it usually stands in our codices, "an *octastyle*, and in the Temple of Jupiter Olympius."

Had the quotation stopped at "Athenis" all would have been clear, but it is impossible to suppose, though all the codices now extant contain it, that Vitruvius inserted the word "octastylos" in this place. He most methodically describes all the forms of temples, according to the number of pillars in their fronts: distyle, tetrastyle, hexastyle, octastyle—two sorts; then proceeds to describe the decastyles and their peculiarities. To assume that he should then have adduced an octastyle temple as an example of a decastyle form is something too absurd. Wilkins suggested the insertion of "in Asty" instead of "octastylos," which has some probability, as in another passage Vitruvius describes the "Olympium in Asty, à Cossutio architectandum." But all suggestions of the sort, in the absence of any statement in any codex, must be mere guesses. The best, it appears, will be one which is in perfect accordance with the context and with what we know of the subject. According to this it will stand: "Sed Athenis *decastylos* est in Templo Olympio." We know that the Temple of Jupiter there was decastyle and dipteral, and had all the peculiarities Vitruvius describes, and it is the only one that existed or exists in Europe which possesses them. It certainly was one of the temples alluded to by Vitruvius, and I believe the only one.

The confusion I believe to have arisen from some over-clever editor, at an early date in the revival of classical literature, seeing that Vitruvius generally quotes two or more examples for his statements, though in this instance only one, changed the "est" into "et,"[1] and decastyle into octastyle, because he knew of a famous octastyle at Athens, and the Temple of Jupiter had lost its decastyle aspect early in the dark ages, and, indeed, never became famous in that character. In so far as any argument based upon it is concerned, it is not the least consequence how the mistake arose, or what the proper correction may be; it is sufficient to know that it is a mistake, because it is in distinct contradiction with another part of the same paragraph, and could not, therefore, be a statement that Vitruvius made in the original text. For our purposes also it is sufficient that he mentions the temple of Olympian Jove as one of the hypæthral temples—if not the only one. This fact is all that we at present are concerned with, and our knowledge of the remains of that temple is sufficient to prove that it contained all the characteristics that he ascribes to hypæthral temples. Whether or not there were others of the same class, is of the least possible consequence for our present purpose. They certainly are not mentioned by Vitruvius.

TEMPLE OF JUPITER OLYMPIUS.

It would add very much to the clearness of what follows if we knew a little more than we do of the history of this celebrated temple, but, like most temples of antiquity, it is only from casual allusions, or fragmentary scraps of information, that we are enabled to piece together what is really known on the subject.

It appears that a great temple on the site was projected by Pisistratus, to replace, it seems, a smaller one, said to have been erected by Deucalion. Owing, however, to the troubles that followed, the design had only been commenced when it was abandoned,[2] and nothing now remains to show what was then intended. From what we know of the architecture of the period at which it was proposed, it probably was intended to be a Greek Doric hexastyle of the first class, like the contemporary temple at Olympia, but, having been designed at Athens, it probably would have far excelled, in beauty of detail at least, that very clumsy specimen of Greek art. Nothing seems to have been done towards its completion during the great age. Pericles—fortunately for us—devoted all the art and all the money at his disposal to the erection of the Parthenon and the Propylæa. The site seems to have been entirely neglected till Antiochus Epiphanes,

---

[1] Schneider, Vitruvius, Notes, vol. ii. p. 179, points out that there is a difference of opinion among commentators whether an "est" or an "et" should be inserted here.
[2] Vitruvius, lib. vii. præfatio.

100 years after its commencement, offered to find the funds necessary for its completion,[1] and, what is more important for our present purposes, employed a Roman architect—Cossutius—to carry out the design. It seems strange that Greek architecture and Greek artists should have been so completely discredited as early as 178 B.C., but so it was, and this temple is consequently really a Roman Corinthian example, though found on Grecian soil. How far, however, the design was carried towards completion, even then, we have no means of knowing. Most probably it was not sufficiently complete to admit of its being consecrated when Sylla removed some of its internal columns, probably of precious marbles, to adorn the Capitol at Rome.[2] That it was not even then quite finished is evident, from a sort of Committee of Kings having met together in the reign of Augustus,[3] to determine what should next be done for its completion. Even they do not seem to have been able to finish it entirely, for, if we may trust Pausanias,[4] it was not dedicated to worship till Hadrian, with his usual magnificence, completed and dedicated the building to the God for whose worship it was originally intended.

Besides the difficulties arising from this imperfect history, we have another, rather unusual at the present day, in the want of any complete and detailed plan of the temple. Owing to the energy and skill of Mr. Penrose, we now know exactly the height and the form of the capitals of the pillars.[5] We also know the position of the 120 pillars of the peristyle, and consequently the general dimensions of the temple, with sufficient accuracy; but when we turn to the interior, except the position of the side-walls—perhaps, too, those at either end—we know nothing. This is mainly due to the obstructiveness of the present Archaeological Society of Athens, who have no means of their own to explore the site, and will allow no one else to do so.[6] The consequence is that we do not know, for a fact, how the interior of the temple was arranged, and can only be guided by our appreciation of how it would best have been done for the general effect of the whole. This, as it happens, is unimportant, in so far as any argument as to the mode of lighting is concerned. The temple was hypæthral, in other words the light was introduced by a great window in an open courtyard, either through the eastern or western wall. Whether the court in front of the window was 50

---

[1] Livy, xli. 20; Vitruvius in loco.
[2] Pliny, Hist. Nat. xxxvi. 5. It is evident it was not the pillars of the peristyle that he removed. Pillars 55 ft. high and 6½ ft. in diameter are not easily put on board ship and carried away; besides there are none such and no place to which they could be applied in the Capitol of Rome.—Pliny's expression is "ex templo."
[3] Suetonius, 60.
[4] Pausanias, I. 18, p. 42; Strabo, ix. 396.
[5] Principles of Athenian Architecture, p. 69, pl. xxxvii. et sqq.
[6] If there were any statues or works of art likely to be found in these excavations their hesitation in allowing foreigners to dig there would be excusable. But as it is only to ascertain the position of the transverse walls of the cella it seems rather a dog-in-the-manger policy not to allow this being ascertained. Nothing would be easier than to ascertain this, but till it is done, Plate No. I. must be considered as a mere diagram to illustrate the text. Any attempt at a real restoration would be labour thrown away, while neither the position of the transverse walls, nor even the orientation of the temple, is ascertained.

feet across, as I believe, or 85, as some may assume, is of little consequence to the argument. Only when attempting the restoration of such a temple as this, you regret being obliged to have recourse to abstract reasoning, when the actual facts of the case could be so easily ascertained.

So little in fact is known with regard to the plan of the temple that it is still uncertain whether the front was turned towards the east or to the west. If we might trust Vitruvius, all temples faced the west,[1] but, like many other assertions of that most unsatisfactory author, we may be allowed to doubt the correctness of them, as applied to Greek temples at all events. The Parthenon, in this immediate neighbourhood, and all the Greek temples whose plans are now known to us, are turned the other way. This one, though built by a Roman, was certainly originally planned by Greek architects, and we have no reason for suspecting that it was turned round in conformity with the western fashion when its completion was undertaken by Cossutius.

1.—Remaining Columns and Temple of Jupiter Olympius at Athens.

In addition to these speculations, however, we know that three ranges of columns existed in front of the antæ at the east end, as shown in the annexed woodcut, which would be appropriate for a pronaos; but such an arrangement is improbable as a posticum, and nowhere exists, so far as we at present know, except in the very exceptional Temple of Diana at Ephesus.[2] Besides this the arch of Hadrian, if the front had been towards the west, would probably have been placed symmetrically in the centre of the front, not diagonally at the corner of the temenos,

---

[1] Vitruvius, lib. iv. chap. v.
[2] The other decastyle dipteral temple whose plan we know so much resembled this one is that at Didymæ. There were there only two ranges of columns in the posticum. It was in fact dipteral behind as on the sides.

as it now stands. But it is needless to waste time in speculating on this, as whenever excavations are allowed, it will be settled in a few minutes with a certainty that no reasoning can replace.

Almost all we know for certainty with regard to the plan of this temple is that it was decastyle, and dipteral, according to Vitruvius's definition of a hypæthral temple, as shown in Plate I.; in other words, that it had 10 columns in front, and two rows of 20 columns on either flank. These seem to have been arranged with an intercolumniation of 18 feet 2 inches from centre to centre of column, making 171 feet in front, by 354 on the flanks, always supposing that the central intercolumniation was the same as the others, which, however, is extremely unlikely. Beyond this we know that the cella was one half of the whole width of the temple, or 86 feet in round numbers, supposing the intercolumniations to be equal, but I fancy 2 or 3 feet must be added from this cause. In the plan, Plate I., I have not ventured to introduce this wider spacing in the centre, though I think it more than probable that it existed.

With regard to the other arrangements of the interior all is conjecture, but so far as I can make out, there was a pronaos 75 feet deep, a vestibule 50 feet in extent leading to a cella 50 feet wide—between the columns,—and 150 feet in length, by 100 feet in height. These are round numbers, of course, but they work out so nearly to what we might expect, that I cannot help fancying that the temple was designed by Cossutius, on some such scheme of regular proportions. I have consequently adopted these dimensions in the plan (Plate I.), which is probably as nearly correct as any plan is likely to be without the necessary examination of the ground by excavation. But these details may safely be left for future determination, whenever the excavations necessary to ascertain them are allowed, and undertaken by any competent explorer.

When I first, in 1848,[1] attempted to restore the temple, I inserted a courtyard in the centre the whole width of the cella, or 86 feet square, surrounded only by a cloister, but left open to the sky in the middle. I did this partly in deference to Vitruvius, "medio autem sub divo et sine tecto," partly because of an analogy I fancied I saw between this, and the atria which almost invariably preceded the Christian Basilicas, and were certainly in some respects copies of the Pagan temples. Subsequent thought and experience have convinced me that this was not the case, at least in this instance, and that a vestibule 50 feet by 86 feet would be infinitely more appropriate. At least I cannot fancy an architectural bathos greater than would occur to a votary on approaching such a temple as this, standing first in a forest of magnificent pillars of the Corinthian order (see last woodcut), and when the doors of the temple are opened, finding himself in an open courtyard or obliged to seek the shelter of a cloister to avoid

[1] True Principles of Beauty in Art. p. 392.

the sun and rain before reaching the real door to a temple of unparalleled magnificence. It was not thus that the Greeks built their temples! On the other hand I would suggest that from the open pronaos he entered into a covered vestibule, which may have been as rich as marbles and mosaics could make it. This, I conceive, was lighted by a sort of clerestory affording a demi-jour from the roof, and then passed into the cella brilliantly lighted from the great east window. I do not know any arrangement in either ancient or modern times more scenic or more artistic. The statue, that this window was designed to illuminate, was, as we learn from Pliny,[1] a chryselephantine statue of Jupiter, probably a copy of the famous one at Olympia. From our knowledge of what the state of the arts was in Hadrian's time it probably was very inferior in point of execution, but it had an immense advantage in position over its rival. At Elis, as we shall presently see, the space in which the statue was placed was so cramped and confined that there is great difficulty in understanding how it could either be advantageously displayed or effectively lighted. Here the spacious and lofty hall in which it was placed, and the perfect mode in which the light was thrown upon it, must have gone far to make up for any inferiority of execution in the statue itself.

On the principle that whatever we can design that is most perfect and most beautiful, is probably nearest to that which the Greeks adopted, we may safely assume that this is more probably what the arrangement of this temple was, than any other which has yet been suggested. This is what I believe Vitruvius intended to describe, when he said that decastyle and dipteral temples were "Medio sub divo et sine tecto." He did not mean that the cella of the temple was without a roof, but that, in the middle of such temples, a space was left without a roof in order that light might by these means be admitted to the great window of the temple, and through it to the cella. His words taken literally will bear perfectly the interpretation here put on them. As usually translated they lead to a "non sequitur," so absurd and monstrous that it may be safely rejected. On any other subject than one connected with the fine arts it would have required the most unqualified assertion and the most detailed description before any one could be brought to believe that the Greeks could not put a water-tight roof over the cella of their temples.

This object was generally easily effected, and in the present instance that the light was introduced by a great window occupying the whole of its eastern or western wall as the case may be, is a proposition so self-evident, it appears to me, as hardly to admit of argument. If any one, after it is pointed out, still cares to adopt the hole in the roof, or to remove the whole of it, as some architects still persist in doing, we have no common ground to stand upon. The one is the most artistic mode of lighting a chamber of this form that has

---

[1] Pliny, lib. xxxiv. chap. viii. p. 587.

yet been invented; the other is artistically the most clumsy, and mechanically the most inconvenient that has yet been adopted even by the most barbarous people. If any one likes to class the Greeks among these, then there is an end of the argument, but believing them to be the most ingenious and most artistic people that ever lived, I approach the question from an entirely different point of view.

The light admitted through such a window as that shown in the diagram (40 ft. by 55 ft.), would of course be in excess of that required in such a climate, especially as that of Athens, to illuminate such an apartment as this cella. But that could be easily remedied. The compartments of the window would be filled with grilles of more or less opacity, and blinds or curtains would be employed, not only to keep out the weather, but to temper the sun's rays, whenever they were likely to prove troublesome. The distance of 50 feet would be more advantageous for this purpose than the 86 originally suggested. It is quite sufficient—as wide as most of our streets—to admit any amount of light, while its contracted width would protect the curtains or blinds from being disturbed by any wind that might tend to derange them. The cella was, of course, surrounded by a range of columns in two stories, "remotas a parietibus," which supported a gallery running all round. This was approached by doorways at either end, in the posticum with the stairs that led to the galleries; but whether these were arranged as I have shown them, or otherwise, will depend on the space that may eventually be found for their accommodation.

The roof I have restored as semicircular—in wood of course—not only because it would be infinitely more beautiful, and in every respect more artistic than a flat ceiling could be made in such a situation; at the same time it is clear that none of the objections, which apply with such force to this mode of roofing

COIN OF GORDIANUS, REPRESENTING THE TEMPLE AT MILETUS.

the temple at Olympia, and the Parthenon, have here any application. On the contrary, the reasoning which Quatremère de Quincy derived from his study of the Roman imperial coins, seems to be conclusive when applied to such a temple as this.[1] In addition to the examples on which he and Mr. Falkener[2] relied for their conclusions, many more have since been brought to light, all bearing more or less directly on the subject, none perhaps more so than the accompanying one from Miletus. It would be almost impossible on a coin to represent more distinctly a section of a dipteral Ionic temple, with the god standing under a semicircular roof; but against this, it may be urged that the temple at Miletus never was roofed, on account of its extent.[3] This

---

[1] Q. de Q. Sur la manière dont étoient éclairés les Temples des Grecs et Romains. Memoires de l'Institut, classe Histoire, vol. iii. 1818. [2] Dædalus, p. 9. [3] Strabo, lib. xiv. p. 634.

may have been true when Strabo wrote, but it by no means follows that it was so when this medal was struck by Gordianus, more than 200 years afterwards. But the most striking illustration of this theory I have met with, is to be found among the coins of the Jews, which bear on the question in a manner that seems unmistakeable.

Before Hadrian's time the architectural coins of the Jews represent either a tetrastyle temple—whatever that may mean—or the beautiful gate of the temple, which we know was spared when the temple itself was destroyed and remained a venerated symbol of its past glories.

"Porta sonet Templi speciosissima quam vocitamus
Egregium Solomonis opus."[1]

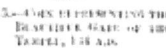

We know from history that Hadrian built a temple at Jerusalem on the site of the temple of the Jews,[2] and from what we know of his buildings we must infer that it had a semicircular roof like that at Baalbec. The Jewish coins

3.—COIN REPRESENTING THE BEAUTIFUL GATE OF THE TEMPLE, 138 A.D.

subsequent to his reign confirm this; nearly all of them represent a nearly similar statue under a simulated vault, with only such variations as might be expected from numismatic representations.[3]

   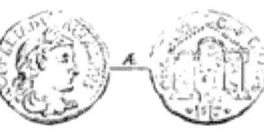

4.—COIN OF HADRIAN.   5.—ANTONINUS PIUS.   6.—PESCENNIUS NIGER.

It is most improbable that the coincidence should be accidental, and it is so thoroughly in accordance with what we know of the architectural history of the age that it nearly amounts to a positive proof that the temple Hadrian built on the site of the Jewish temple had a semicircular roof, and strongly supports the probability of these coins really being intended to represent temples so roofed.

This temple disappeared about the time of Constantine, probably was pulled down by him, to supply materials for his Church of the Holy Sepulchre, now known as the Mosque of Omar. At least we cannot see whence he obtained the shafts of precious marbles with which that edifice is adorned, unless it was from some temple of Imperial Rome, which used them as ornaments as no other builders did either before or afterwards.

---

[1] Aurelius Prudentius, Diss. xlvi. circa 407 A.D.

[2] Bordeaux Pilgrim; Tobler, Palestina, pp. 3 and 4; Hieron, Com in Isaiam; Vals sius, vol. iv. p. 57.

[3] I am indebted to the liberality of Mr. Trübner for the clichés of these four coins from Madden's Coins of the Jews in the 'Numismata Orientalia.' There are four or five others similar, but these are sufficient to illustrate the types, and there are I believe many similar coins, as Mr. Madden by no means pretends to have exhausted this branch of the subject, but these are sufficient for our present purposes.

No one at the present day will probably be found objecting that the arch was not then currently used, and was not therefore likely to be adopted as an architectural form, at that time. It was a very favourite mode of construction with the Etruscans in all ages, and the Cloaca Maxima at Rome, which certainly was constructed in the time of the kings, is as perfect a specimen of arch construction as has been produced since that time. But even before their time it certainly was employed as an architectural feature by the Egyptians. They seem to have used arches, and for architectural purposes, from a very early age. The tombs at Beni Hassan, of the twelfth dynasty, show segmental roofs, copied evidently from forms that could only be suggested by arch construction (probably in brick). But one of the most striking examples is in the Temple of Rhamses II. at Abydos. In it there are seven cells, each 17 feet 6 inches wide by 34 feet in length, all of which have simulated arched roofs; not, it is true, real constructive arches, but large masses of stone cut away to imitate these forms. Men must have been long familiar with it, and thought it—partly in consequence—the most beautiful form of roof, before they would have gone to the expense of shaping great blocks, and "pro tanto" weakening them, by removing the parts most important for strength before employing them in masonry. But besides this one, there are many other examples in Egypt of the practical employment of arched forms in architectural decoration—so numerous, indeed, as to prove that both the Greeks and Romans must early have been familiar with its appearance, whether they adopted it or not in the temple roofs.

It is hardly to be expected that architects who have only studied this art in Europe, should either understand the properties, or appreciate the artistic value, of this mode of introducing light into temples. There are no examples existing where its effects can be observed or its details studied in a satisfactory manner. It would be easy, of course, to make a model, and, if on a sufficient scale, its effect might be shown without much difficulty; but among the very few persons who might be induced to look at such a model, there is probably hardly one who would devote to it the time that might be requisite to master the details, or to assure himself of the probability of its ever having been carried into execution. "Ingenious, but not probable," would probably be the verdict on the model, as it will most likely be on this chapter, and it is hardly worth the trouble of obtaining such a verdict, especially if thoughtlessly delivered.

When, however, Indian architecture comes to be studied with more care, means will be available which may bring this mode of lighting within the range of reasonable probabilities, inasmuch as there are in India at least twenty to thirty cave-temples which are all lighted in this manner. Many of these are now so ruined, that the effect of their mode of lighting cannot be seen, but others are so complete, even in the present day, that the result may be seen almost as perfectly as when first excavated.

Among these, the finest and best preserved, as it happens, is the great cave at Karlé, which has also the advantage for present purposes of being of about the same age as the Temple of Jupiter Olympius, having been excavated probably in the first century before Christ, and also because it is not dissimilar in dimensions. The nave, it is true, is only about half the width—25 feet against 50—between the pillars, and only 45 feet between the walls. But the image is nearly at the same distance from the window—about 100 feet—which is far more important for our present purposes. In this instance in India the principal object of worship is a

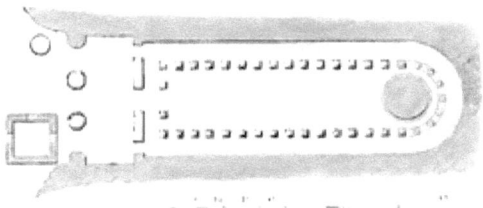

7.—PLAN OF THE CAVE TEMPLE AT KARLÉ.

dagoba, or simulated relic-shrine, which, when perfect, was covered by elaborately carved wood-work, and surmounted by one or three umbrellas of a very ornamental character—probably the whole heightened by colour to a very considerable extent. But, however this may be, it formed a very similar object, both in size and richness, to the colossal chryselephantine statue of Jupiter, which occupied a similar position in the temple. The light was introduced into the cave through one great horse-shoe window, about 20 feet in height, and about the same width.

8.—SECTION OF THE CHAITYA TEMPLE AT KARLÉ. (Scale 50 feet to 1 inch.)

which in that climate was felt to be excessive. It was consequently subdued, first by an open screen of wood-work in the arch of the window itself, but more so by a great framework of wood erected in front, which almost entirely hid the great window from view externally. In consequence of this arrangement, the votary approaching the Chaitya saw only the richly-ornamented detached façade of the cave, and passed on till he stood in comparative gloom in the entrance, when the whole glory of the richly-ornamented colonnade, and more richly-adorned dagoba, burst upon him. The whole interior was thus bathed in a flood of light, the origin of which he could not see, but which was more than sufficient to illuminate all the essential parts of the temple, leaving all beyond in illimitable gloom. I have seen all this, and can answer for it, that the effect is magical, and no mode of lighting which is to be seen anywhere equals it in scenic perfection.

If this were the proper place to argue it, it would be an interesting question to try and ascertain whether this mode of lighting was an independent invention on the part of the Indians, or whether they borrowed it from Western temples. My own impression is that the latter hypothesis is very much more likely to repre-

7.—View of the Interior of the Chaitya Temple at Karli. (From a Photograph.)

sent the true state of the case. After the glorious raid of Alexander and the establishment of the Bactrian kingdom, the Indian architects must have had abundant opportunities of observing how the Western nations lighted their temples, while it is quite certain that they had no stone architecture of their own, anterior to the reign of Asoka (B.C. 250). It is consequently very unlikely they would have invented so simple a mode, and one so adapted to stone architecture, without some foreign suggestion. The temptation in wooden architecture is to introduce light anyhow and everywhere, it is so easily done; but the simplicity of one great window seems foreign to its spirit, and would hardly have been adopted in such buildings as those from which we know the Chaitya caves were literally copied.

None of these wooden buildings, of course, now exist, but all the Chaitya caves excavated before the Christian era are such literal copies of wooden buildings, as to prove that the people that erected them had no knowledge of stone architecture, for we cannot detect one lithic form in any part of their temples. It may have been that the admirable adaptability for the purpose of temples lighted from the front only, first suggested the use of this form of cave architecture; and it is also curious that it is only found in a limited district in the west of India, where we may suppose the influence of Greek or Roman architecture would be especially felt.[1] This, however, is a digression, and though an interesting one, which may some day lead to curious evidence of the relations that existed in those times between the West and the East, is not of special importance to the question we are now discussing. These Indian cave-temples are quoted here, only as full-sized models to exemplify the mode in which light was introduced into such a temple as that of Jupiter Olympius at Athens; and when they are used for that purpose no one, I think, that looks on them with the eye of an artist, but must admit that it is one of the most perfect modes of lighting which has yet been invented or introduced anywhere.[2]

It may strike some as strange that if this mode of lighting was so perfect and so generally adopted as we believe it to have been in pagan temples, no trace of it is found in any of the earlier Christian churches, or, indeed, in those of any age. A little acquaintance with the architectural history of the period will easily explain this. The early Christians rarely, if ever, adopted the temples of their predecessors as places of worship. They hated and abhorred them, and this is one of the causes why so few have been preserved to the present day. The regal basilica was the form of edifice they copied for all their larger churches, the domestic room sufficed as a model for their smaller chapels. In them the light was introduced anywhere, in such quantities as was required, without an attempt at artistic effect, and long before they were capable of glazing such an opening as above described, painted glass had begun to exert its influence. The window, instead of being used for the purpose of introducing light in the best possible manner, became itself a principal ornament, to which its primitive function of admitting light was only a secondary consideration. It perhaps would be too much to assert that there is not a single instance of artistic lighting, or any attempt at it, in any building in the middle ages. A wall of coloured glass was all that was required, through which a sufficiency of light struggled to render objects sufficiently visible for the purposes of the building, but nowhere was this so arranged as to throw a blaze of light on any part of the building or any object in it. There is a glory about these

---

[1] A good deal was said about this mode of lighting in my work on the Rock-Cut Temples of India, p. 35 et seq., published 1845, but it is treated of in more detail and with fuller illustrations in a book on the Cave Temples of India, by myself conjointly with Mr. Burgess, published in 1880 for the Government of India.

[2] See also Yule's Mission to the Court of Ava, p. 48, Fig. 18.

walls of painted glass that may well induce us to overlook this defect; but while we have gone back to the employment of white glass, it is strange that no one has ever thought, especially in our churches, how an effect might be produced by white light artistically introduced.

There are other points connected with the mode of lighting which will be frequently adverted to in the sequel, but enough has been probably said to prove that the Temple of Jupiter Olympius at Athens was, as Vitruvius tells us, an hypæthral temple, and that it possesses every one of the characteristics which he describes as belonging to temples of that class. At the same time it admitted of being lighted by as perfect a system of illumination as has been devised by any architect in any part of the world.

This is all that is required for the more direct purposes of this work. If it is admitted that the above is a correct description of the mode in which light was admitted to this temple, the passage in Vitruvius which has hitherto proved such a stumbling-block to commentators is so no longer. An hypæthral temple, or one "medio sub divo et sine tecto," no longer means a temple without a roof and exposed to all the inclemencies of the climate, whatever these may have been. On the contrary, it means a temple as perfectly protected from the weather as any temple could be before the invention and use of glass, and lighted in the most perfect manner which human ingenuity has yet devised.

Temple at Samos

Besides the great temple of Jupiter Olympius at Athens, there are only three temples in the ancient world which can claim to be ranked as hypæthral temples, according to the definition of them contained in the works of Vitruvius. All three are situated in Asia Minor, and very near to one another.

Of these the earliest—in its decastyle form at least—appears to be that of Samos, described by Herodotus as the largest he was acquainted with, and as built by Rhæcus, the son of Phila, a Samian.[1]

In 1812 a commission from the Dilettanti Society, consisting of Sir W. Gell, Messrs. Bedford and Gandy, visited the spot, though without apparently attempting any excavation. They arrived at the conclusion that the temple was decastyle and dipteral, measuring 164 feet in front by 344 feet on the flank, which is probably an under-estimate, from their not having taken into account the half diameter of the columns at the angles.[2] Subsequently it was examined, but again without excavation, with nearly the same result, by M. Paul Girard, a French architect. He makes the extent of the front about 165 feet, but found it impossible to ascertain its other dimensions.[3]

It is much to be regretted that no thorough exploration of the temple, by

---

[1] Herodotus, lib. iii. 60, ii. 148 and i. 70.
[2] Antiquities of Ionia, vol. i. chap. v. p. 64.
[3] Bulletin de correspondence Hellénique, Athens, June 1880, p. 384, 94.

excavation, has been attempted, not only because, if the internal arrangements could be discovered, it might throw considerable light on the early form of the hyperthron, but because its architecture, though not beautiful, is abnormal, and might elucidate some problems which now remain obscure. In the plates published by the Dilettanti Society, several of the bases are figured, which are entirely unlike any found elsewhere. There is no plinth, but in its place a circular drum, with a number of nearly equal grooves or sinkings, and above this a torus moulding equally grooved, with a singular want of grace and elegance. The pillar too, if the drawing is to be trusted (Plate II.), is without entasis, but narrows at the top in a very unusual manner, and the capital is ornamented with a circle of ovolos of a rather peculiar character. From their appearance it has been generally assumed that the temple was Ionic, but without any material evidence of the fact. There are no volutes anywhere, nor is it easy to see how any could be fitted to this capital, while, on the other hand, we have the assertion of Vitruvius most deliberately expressed that the Temple was Doric.[1]

There is nothing at present known to contradict this. If, of course, we understand Greek Doric, the assertion is absurd, but there is some reason for supposing that another form of Doric may have existed in former times from which the Roman order sprang. There is some reason to suspect that it was not derived direct from the Greek order, and if so, the exploration of this temple might open up a new chapter in the history of architecture, besides explaining many passages in Vitruvius which at present sound mysterious. Why, for instance, should some architects contend that the Doric order was not suited to sacred edifices, while the Greeks employed no other; and why and how did Hermogenes convert the material he had prepared for a Doric temple at Teos into one of the Ionic order? If we may consider the temple at Samos as Doric the answer is easy, though with a Greek Doric order the connection seems impossible.[2] All this, however, is mere speculation, based on very insufficient evidence. A few days' excavation may upset it all, but it is introduced here to point out peculiarities which may be overlooked or not sought for, and for the purpose of directing attention to some assertions of Vitruvius, which have hitherto been inexplicable.

There are two or three coins representing this temple with a circular roof—supposing that theory to be admitted—one quoted by Professor Donaldson[3] is one of the finest of its class, but strange to say the deity represented is certainly not Juno, but Artemis of Ephesus, and how this transposition was made is by no means clear. On the same plate, however, Mr. Donaldson quotes another coin (No. 23) which shows the temple with a straight-lined pediment, which so far as it goes tends to invalidate the theory of the arched form indicating a circular roof.

---

[1] "Posten. Sil ans de symmetris Doricorum edidit volumen; de æde Junonis quae est Sami Dorica; Theodorus de Ionica Ephesi, quae est Dianae Chersiphrones Metagenes," &c., præf. lib. xii.

[2] Vitruvius, lib. iv. ch. iii. beginning.

[3] Architectura Numismatica, No. 22.

Curiously enough the goddess in this instance, as in the other, is not the Samian Juno, but the Ephesian Artemis, as shown in No. 6 of the same work.

All this is hazy and unsatisfactory, but only renders it the more evident how desirable it is that some scientific exploration of the temple should be undertaken as soon as possible. It is strange that with all these inducements to explore it, the French or German Governments have never undertaken the examination of this temple. Even the Americans, who are now distinguishing themselves in this line, would certainly find here a more profitable field of exploration than at Assos. Till some private enterprise undertakes it, our apathetic Government will not interfere, but it is hoped that before long something may be done by others, as nothing appears to be so easy. The site of the temple is perfectly well known, one pillar is still standing erect. The plan is at least approximately known—it is not encumbered by any houses, and is only buried under the soil to a very slight extent. The last indeed is a most unfavourable point. It is hardly probable that the natives will have left much unutilized, but it may be that much still remains, at least it is, at all events, worth trying.

DIDYME.

The second hypæthral temple in Asia is that of Apollo at Didyme, near Miletus, where enough remains to make its external arrangement quite certain. It possesses all the characteristics of a perfect hypæthral temple: it is decastyle and dipteral, and its dimensions are of the first class—163 feet in front, and 366 in the flanks, with its 120 columns disposed almost exactly as those are in the Temple of Jupiter Olympius at Athens, except only that it has twelve pillars in the pronaos instead of eight as in that example. In other respects the two plans are so nearly identical, that they might be superimposed without one being able to detect much difference between them, a circumstance of considerable importance to us in determining the external arrangements of the Athenian temple. That at Didyme was existing when Cossutius was called upon to complete that of Jupiter, under the patronage of Antiochus Epiphanes. The number of ascertained points of resemblance, both in dimension and arrangement, is a strong presumption that the disposition of the one was copied from that of the other. The known differences, too, seem to be improvements on the older temple. The disposition of the columns of the front at Athens seems a decided advance in design on the enormously deep pronaos at Didyme; and, if I am correct, the wider hypæthron is also a decided improvement, if the internal disposition of the two temples was what I suppose them to have been. This, however, is at present too uncertain to found any argument upon it.

When, however, from the external disposition of the columns, we turn to the

---

A statue has recently been added to the Louvre collection, said to come from Samos. It is certainly the most archaic—probably the oldest Greek statue known to exist. The head is wanting, but it appears to be of Juno.

Ant. of Ionia, vol. i. pl. iv. ch. iii. Rayet and Thomas, Gazette des Beaux Arts, Juillet, 1876.

interior, the case is widely different, and we are forced to confess that nothing is known with certainty. Messrs. Rayet and Thomas made some excavations—under great difficulties—in 1876, but without any satisfactory result. The place was encumbered with habitations, especially an important windmill, that stood on a mound, composed of the mass of the ruins of the pronaos. In the cella they found that the place had been at one time occupied, as at Ephesus, by a Christian church, and the original pagan arrangements were in consequence hopelessly disturbed or obliterated. Under these circumstances, their explorations have added little to our stock of information, or to our knowledge of the internal arrangements, and this, it must be confessed, was especially scant.

Diodorus, who is one of the few authors who describes the temple from personal observation, says that it was not roofed, in consequence of its largeness,¹ which was, no doubt, true when he saw it, but it is absurd to suppose that any Greek architect designed such a temple, without knowing beforehand how it could be, and was intended to be covered, especially as there was not any special difficulty in the case. The cella was only 70 feet wide between the pilasters, the same as that at Ephesus, which we know was roofed, and less than that of Jupiter Olympius at Athens, regarding which we never heard of there being any difficulty. Besides this, the normal ordinance of a hypæthral temple is to have "columnas remotas a parietibus," which enabled the architect to divide his naos or nave into three aisles, in any proportion he thought most expedient. Forty feet, with two aisles of 15 feet each, would be a very easy task, but from two offsets in the western wall, it seems 50 feet by 10 was that which was adopted, and, with a vaulted roof, nothing would have been easier for a Greek architect. In front of the cella there is a space left as a vestibule or hypæthron, of 30 feet in width, which—when I previously attempted the restoration of the temple² —did not appear to me sufficient for the purpose, if the whole of the cella was roofed over, and depended for its light on this one opening. I consequently proposed to cut off the last 50 feet for the accommodation of the oracle, which was certainly in the open part, as the oracle was under a sacred laurel, or grove of laurels,³ which could not have grown except in the open air.

If no other evidence were available, the coin of Gordianus, above quoted (p. 22), is sufficient, I fancy, to prove that, at one time, the temple had a roof, but how to fit it to the existing remains must remain a problem, till a more complete exploration of the temple is made than Messrs. Rayet and Thomas, with their limited means, and with the time at their disposal, were enabled to effect; or till at least the results of their exploration are published. All we know of them at present is in a short article in the 'Gazette des Beaux Arts,' 1876, but it is understood a thoroughly scientific account is in preparation, and may presently appear. Till it does, any attempt to restore this temple or describe its internal

---

¹ Διέφυγε δὲ χωρὶς ἐροφῆς διὰ τὸ μέγεθος. Lib. iv. ch. i. 634.   ² Sessional Papers, Institute of Brit. Arch. 1877.   ³ Diodorus, loc. cit.

disposition, must be hazardous in the extreme, and of very little use to any one. I am afraid, however, from what I have seen of the plates of their work, that it will throw very little light on the original internal disposition of this famous temple.

DIANA AT EPHESUS.

The third of these great Asiatic hypæthrals is the most interesting of any, and was by the ancients themselves considered as one of the wonders of the world, and, so far as we can judge of its original form from the recently-discovered remains, not without good reason.

All we really know about this far-famed Temple of Diana of the Ephesians is due to the indomitable courage and perseverance of J. T. Wood, who not only discovered the long-lost temple, but during eleven whole years, in spite of every possible discouragement, persevered till he had scraped the foundations bare, and brought away all the available remains, and all the information that can now be obtained regarding it. Unfortunately all he has yet told us regarding these remarkable explorations is contained in a volume published by Longmans in 1877, giving a popular account of his experiences, but with the fewest possible facts with regard to the temple conveyed in the most unscientific manner.[1]

Mr. Wood was fortunate in finding the bases of two pillars *in situ* in exactly the position most useful for determining the main features of the peristyle. Even more important than this, however, was the discovery of nearly a hundred feet of the lowest step of the podium on the northern side, which enabled him to ascertain the width of the pyramid of steps about 10 feet in height, on which it was known the temple was raised, and which, in fact, from its highly ornamental character, formed the principal glory of the fane.

---

[1] When I first took up the idea of restoring this temple, in the paper I laid before the Royal Institute of British Architects in 1877, I was so impressed with the notion that Mr. Wood had discovered and knew all that was to be known about this temple, that I did not dream of questioning the statements as found in his book. My task I believed to be to fit my theories to his facts, and to that alone I applied myself. Subsequent experience has convinced me that his views with regard to the restoration of the temple are erroneous in every essential respect. As he persistently declines to publish the results of his excavations in an intelligible form, he has consequently as yet, except in details, added very little to the knowledge we previously possessed. His refusal to do so is understood to be based on the idea that he may one day be able to publish a great work on the subject himself. The unsuccessful result, however, of his popular work, in a pecuniary sense, is not likely to encourage any bookseller to undertake so unprofitable a speculation; while he has not yet earned any such position from his knowledge of the principles or theory of Greek art as would encourage any Society to enlist his services. Meanwhile, he refuses to allow even the Trustees of the British Museum, who have spent some £16,000 on the excavations, to have even a tracing of his working plan, on the plea that he was not a regular paid servant of the Government, and that consequently any information he might obtain was his own private property. Legally he may be right, but it is a pity when legal rights are used to withhold information to which the public are morally entitled. It would cost the merest trifle to put the working plan on stone by photography, and we should all then have some authentic data to work from; at present we have nothing but a "popular" plan on too small a scale to be of much value.

He also found, what he supposed to be, a step 10 feet in length on its eastern face, at a distance of about 35 feet from his peristyle,[1] which he assumed to be a continuation of that on the northern side, and therefore the limit of the podium on that side. There is, however, nothing whatever to show that this was so, or that it may not have belonged to one of the two preceding temples which we know were erected on the same spot and with nearly the same dimensions, if indeed it is *in situ*, which is by no means clear. But, however this may be, no fancied discovery of Mr. Wood's, or any one else, can, I conceive, weigh for one moment against the deliberate assertion of Pliny, expressed in words, that this temple had one hundred and twenty-seven columns.[2] Whatever may have been the case with the temple built and described by Chersiphrones and Metagenes,[3] there can be little doubt but that the enlarged temple built by Cheiromocrates[4] after it was burnt by Herostratus, had that number of columns. The numerous details of the arrangements and measurements of that temple given by Pliny[5] is a sufficient proof that he must have had a written description of it before him, from which he was quoting what we now find is compatible with the most minute accuracy. It is true the odd number has hitherto proved a stumbling-block to restorers. Mr. Falkener proposes to insert a comma after 120,[6] so making that the number. Mr. Wood gets over the difficulty by a stop after "centum," thus assuming 100 was the number. It is always dangerous, however, to tamper with the text of an author when there is nothing in the context to lead any one to suppose an error existed, and any restoration based only on the arbitrary insertion of commas, where none existed, or other alterations of an established text, can only be regarded as confession of inability to read the text aright, and is consequently of slight value from a scientific point of view. When, however, the thing is fairly looked at, it is easy to see that 127 was the number which really existed.

No temple in the ancient world had so essentially a front and a back as that at Ephesus. The western front faced the city and the port. The eastern was hidden by a hill, on the slope of which it rested. All the art of the architect was consequently lavished on the western front. The central intercolumniation was of the unusual extent of 29 feet from centre to centre of the columns; so large, indeed, that the architect despaired of ever being able to place so large an architrave in such a situation, and determined in consequence on committing suicide. Before, however, it was too late the goddess appeared to him in a dream and bid him not despair, and when he awoke in the morning he found the lintel in position placed there by the goddess herself.[7] Besides this wonderful central intercolumniation, there is a graduated spacing towards the flanks, which is found in only one other

---

[1] Neither of these steps is shown on any plan published by him, but they are marked on that which accompanied my lecture in 1877, from a MS. plan by him.

[2] Pliny, lib. xxxvi. 11.
[3] Vitruvius, lib. vii. in præf.
[4] Strabo, lib. xiv. p. 640.   [5] Pliny, loc. cit.
[6] Ephesus, p. 241.   [7] Pliny, loc. cit.

temple in the ancient world,[1] that of Cybele at Sardis. The spaces at Ephesus next the centre were 23 feet 6 inches, the next 20 feet, and the remaining pair 19 feet.

It might be worth while incurring these difficulties, which were no doubt appropriate for the principal front of a great temple, but it by no means follows that the rear must be so treated. There the builders got over the difficulty of the wide central intercolumniation, and also of the side ones, by introducing a central pillar. This was no unusual feature in Greek architecture. There is a temple or hall with a portico of nine pillars at Paestum, and the great temple at Agrigentum has seven pillars on each face, and there may have been many others so treated. With this most probable rectification we have instead of the wide-spaced octastyle portico on the west, a reasonable one of nine pillars on the east, the central five being spaced as nearly as possible 19 feet apart, from centre to centre, which is almost exactly the intercolumniation Mr. Wood found had been used in all the angles of the building, and therefore the one most probably employed in this position.

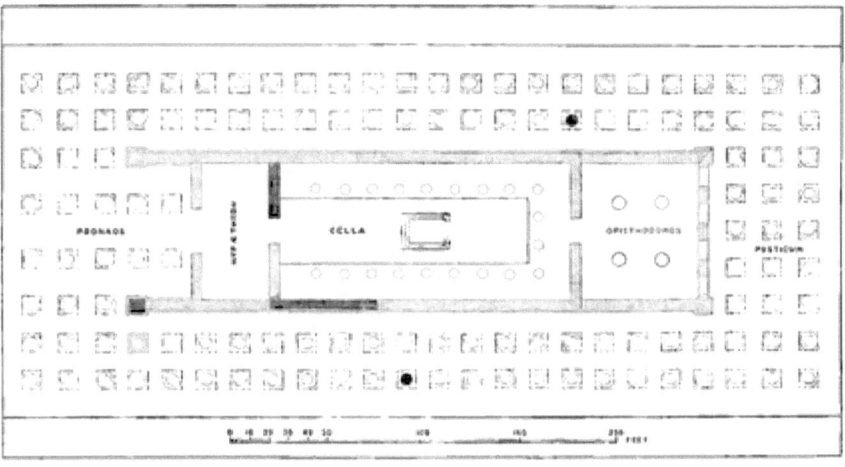

10.—Diagram showing the Arrangement of the 127 Columns of the Temple at Ephesus.

Assuming this porch to have been composed of three rows of pillars it gives the twenty-seven we are looking for (3 times 9 = 27). For the remaining 100 we have only to add another range to the western porch, and add two pillars to the pronaos, which can be done in perfect accordance with all Mr. Wood discovered there, and the

---

[1] Vide Cockerell. Appendix to Leake's Travels in Asia Minor.

tale is made up of 127 in perfect accordance, it appears to me, with all the principles of Greek architecture, and with all we know of this wonderful temple.

We learn from Pliny that all the columns of the peristyle were 60 Greek feet in height, and according to this arrangement of them, they extended to 410 feet English, which allows 10 feet on either front for the flight of steps that led up to it, so as to make up the 425 Greek feet, which Pliny specifies as the length of the temple. As this measurement belongs to the "universum templum" it was certainly measured on the third step from the base, and may therefore be looked upon as singularly confirmative of the restoration now proposed. There is no difficulty with regard to the transverse section of 220 Greek feet, as explained in my Paper read to the Royal Institute of British Architects in 1877, to which the reader is referred for further details of this podium.

Perhaps the most brilliant result of Mr. Wood's excavation was the discovery of several of the drums of the "columnae celatae," thirty-six of which Pliny informs us adorned the peristyle of this temple. Till the fragments which are now in the British Museum were brought to light, the expression in Pliny was unintelligible, no such feature being found anywhere else. With regard to the circular drums there is no possibility of doubt, but Mr. Wood seems to have been mistaken with respect to some rectilinear fragments which he assumed were part of the frieze of the temple, but seem almost certainly to be part of square bases, on which some at least of these circular drums were mounted.[1]

11.—Proposed Restoration of One of the Sculptured Columns at Ephesus.

[1] From the evidence of the stones brought home, as well as from his own admission, it seems perfectly clear that those fragments which he supposed belonged to the frieze, are in reality portions of square pedestals on which some —we probably shall never know how many—of the "columnae celatae" were raised. Among the traditions preserved by Pliny, is one, that Scopas himself sculptured one of these columns. To assume that he would condescend to carve one of these decorative bases like those in the British Museum seems most unlikely; but a square base, like that I have suggested, might have afforded a scope worthy of his reputation.

The practice of raising columns on pedestals was by no means an unusual one, at least in Roman times. We have, of course, no contemporary example to compare with these, but we know from photographs that at Kenawat and Mousmieh we have examples in

It may appear strange that no fragment of the frieze of the temple was found in the excavations, as it is almost impossible to conceive such a temple without such an ornament, and a plain frieze would have been in singular discord with the sculptured drums of the lower part of the columns. The thin slabs, however, of which it certainly was composed, were more easily broken up and turned to use as lime than any other part of the peristyle, and may easily have been all so utilized; or, more probably, the sculpture of the frieze was in bronze, which would accord better with what I conceive to be the style of the podium, and, like everything in metal, would easily have disappeared.

The evidence is very far from being so complete as might be desired or

the first and second centuries which architecturally resemble these in almost all respects. These evidently were copied from previously existing examples.

17.—BASE OF COLUMN AT KENAWAT. (From a Photograph.)

The principal proof that they are not parts of the frieze is that four, if not five of them, show traces of sculpture on two faces. If, consequently, they belonged to the frieze, we possess in the Museum the four angles, and not one fragment of the intermediate parts of the frieze, which is a coincidence that is most improbable, not to say impossible. The evidence that they are bases consists mainly in the fact that two of them at least show the marks of circular drums on their summit. There is, it must be admitted, some little difficulty in fitting the drums to the lower parts in the Museum specimens, as shown in woodcut No. 14. Some

member seems wanting. As originally designed their superposition was probably more like that used at Kenawat, as represented in the next woodcut.

During his excavations, Mr. Wood found a sculptured drum that was considerably less in diameter than the others, being only 5 feet 6 inches in diameter, instead of 6 feet, which is that of all the others found ('Discoveries at Ephesus,' p. 266). In order to account for this anomaly, he assumed that, in some instances, three sculptured drums were placed over one another; and so he represents all those on the east front of the temple. This would, no doubt, account for the diminution; but it appears so clumsy and inartistic an expedient, that we can hardly conceive it being adopted. If, on the other hand, we assume that some of the pillars were mounted on square bases, which the fragments in the Museum seem to prove was certainly the case, we get over the difficulty in a much more artistic manner. The result in that case would be something like that represented in woodcut No. 14, which seems to be a great improvement on that suggested by Mr. Wood.

The one question that concerns us now is how many were so treated, and where were they placed. When I last (in 1877) attempted to restore this temple,* I placed four in the pronaos and four in the posticum. On second thoughts, having reference (especially to what occurred at Didyme) and a more careful study of the meagre details of Mr. Wood's book, I am inclined to believe that all the eight columns of the west front were so adorned, and three or more of the central ones on the east front.†

---

* Sessional Papers, R.I.B.A. Jan. 1877.
† When Mr. Wood informs us where the fragments now in the British Museum were found, we shall be in a better position to speak on the subject.

expected with regard to the disposition of the interior. When I before attempted to restore the temple I accepted Mr. Wood's disposition of the interior in all its main features, thinking that he must have had authority for them; only, finding that he placed two dark vestibules at either end of the cella, carefully roofing over these and unroofing the cella, I reversed the disposition, which admitted more than sufficient light to the sanctuary, while affording a reasonable explanation for all the parts.[1] On a more careful examination of the evidence I find that there is no authority whatever for the opisthodomos of Mr. Wood. The cella wall on either side has been carefully examined for its whole length, and shows no evidence of any transverse wall for the length of 150 feet from the western wall, the position of which is perfectly ascertained. There was however an offset at the eastern end on either side at that distance and 75 feet from his exterior. It is rendered more probable that this was so, from the fact that a platform for the altar, 20 feet in extent, was found in the centre of this space, 65 feet from either end, and the statue of the goddess was then probably placed 20 feet behind this, or about 100 feet from the great window. This was a very probable arrangement, and is quite near enough to the light, especially as the statue was not a work of art dependent on the mode of lighting for its artistic effect, but a "simulacrum," whose effect would be aided by partial obscurity. However this may be, as the evidence at present stands the cella of the temple at Ephesus was a great hall 70 feet wide by 150 in length; or between the pillars 40 feet by 120. The roof seems to have been constructed with lacunaria of cedar,[2] almost certainly in the form of a semicircular vault, and lighted, as the Temple of Jupiter Olympius at Athens was, by one great window at the west end.

One of the most satisfactory results from this arrangement of the peristyle, is that it admits of the introduction of an opisthodomos, worthy of the temple, without interfering in any way with the cella. Assuming the latter to have been 150 feet long, this seems to have been a magnificent apartment, measuring 70 feet by 60, with a flat ceiling supported by four pillars. It was approached apparently from the peristyle by two doors—there may have been four—and was lighted in all probability by four honest windows in the upper part of its eastern wall, similar to those found in the Erechtheum at Athens, or the great temple at Agrigentum, with which this temple has much in common.

The glory of the Ephesian temple did not consist so much in its peristyle of 127 columns, even with its "columnae celatae," as in its base or podium, 10 feet in height — the "Universum Templum," of Pliny, which must have been arranged in the most artistic manner, and adorned with sculpture of the most elaborate character. Mr. Wood's plain flight of steps certainly does not in any way

[1] Sessional Papers, R.I.B.A., 1877.
[2] It would, of course, be quite out of place to enter on any disquisition of the disputed points, or attempt any description of the temple in this place. It is only introduced here in order to explain the mode in which light was introduced into its interior, and so only that it may be classed among the hypæthral temples as described by Vitruvius. I hope some day to attempt a more careful restoration.

represent this wonder-work. In 1877 I tried to work out something more in accordance with the style and character of the temple, but the paucity of the data prevented my arriving at anything like certainty. It is to that part, however, that the measurements quoted by Pliny certainly apply—not to the peristyle—and to this, whoever in future attempts to restore the temple, will find it necessary to apply all his skill and ingenuity, to make it worthy of being one of the wonders of the world.

So far as our present knowledge extends it appears that the temples of Juno at Samos, Apollo at Didyme, Diana at Ephesus, and Jupiter Olympius at Athens, form in themselves a group apart, different from all others in the ancient world. The Temple of Cybele at Sardis comes next, not in dimensions it is true, but in disposition. The great temples at Agrigentum and Selinus equal them in size, but are so totally different from them in design that no comparison can be made between them. The four are, however, so alike in their disposition, in the number of pillars in the peristyles, and in other peculiarities, that they may be treated as much as a class as thirteenth-century cathedrals in France. What is predicated of one may be said of all four, with very slight variations. Fortunately Vitruvius mentions some of the most striking peculiarities of one of the group, which we now find is applicable to all four, and with this hint we are now enabled to restore them all without much uncertainty. When that of Samos is explored, and when M. Rayet publishes what was found at Didyme, we may arrive still nearer the truth. But pending that, my impression is, that Plate I. contains all the requisite elements of a satisfactory restoration of these hypæthral temples. All that is wanted to reduce the whole to a certainty is that the Greeks should allow the transverse walls of the cella of the Temple of Jupiter to be examined, that Messrs. Rayet and Thomas should publish the result of their exploration, and that Mr. Wood should let us know what the results of his excavations really were. A very short time would be amply sufficient to do all this, but the subject is of so little general interest that some time may elapse before all the information is given to the public which will settle all the collateral subjects on a satisfactory basis. In the meanwhile, in so far as the main purpose of this book is concerned, it is of the least possible consequence. The four temples are the only ones we know of as existing in the ancient world which come under the designation of hypæthral temples, according to Vitruvius, and they are so alike in all their arrangements that we may feel certain that what can be predicated of the one can almost certainly be said of all. If, therefore, the description is correct of the mode in which light was introduced into the Temple of Jupiter Olympius in Athens, as shown in Plate I., it is nearly certain that it was the mode—"mutatis mutandis"—which was adopted in the other three. If this is so, it is evident we can afford to wait, in so far as regards the main object of their being mentioned here, for any reasonable time. It would be satisfactory to know more, but in so far as the mode of lighting is concerned, the example of Jupiter Olympius is sufficient.

CHAPTER II.

PSEUDO-HYPÆTHRAL TEMPLES.

In the preceding chapter, and the paper laid before the Royal Institute of British Architects in 1877, it has been attempted to show what Vitruvius really meant by the expression "hypæthral temple," and how that mode of introducing light was practised by the ancients. The description, it must be admitted, does not amount to a mathematical demonstration. No one, indeed, who is familiar with the condition of ruin in which the buildings exist, or with the unsatisfactory state of the literature of the subject, would expect that it should do so. But on the principle that what we can conceive to be artistically and mechanically most perfect, was the mode most likely to be adopted by the ancients, the theory acquires, to say the least of it, a strong degree of probability. When to this we add such indications as can be gathered from the buildings or books, it appears as certain as anything of the sort can well be, and may at least be adopted till some more plausible theory is suggested. If this is so, it would appear strange if, after inventing and using so perfect a mode of lighting their temples, the ancients had suddenly abandoned it, and either reverted to darkness or some less artistic mode of introducing light. But the question here arises, did they? My own conviction is that the Romans practised this mode of lighting in a modified form down to the fall of Paganism, and applied it uniformly to all these great semicircular roofed or vaulted temples for which it was so peculiarly adapted. The difficulty of proving this is the same as in everything else connected with them, that all are so completely ruined. A semicircular vault is even more liable to be destroyed by atmospheric influences than a pointed one, and once the wooden protection is removed, their fall is almost inevitable, besides, as the Hindus say, "an arch never sleeps;" and once from any cause the abutments are removed or weakened, a collapse is inevitable.

There is, so far as I know, only one temple in the Roman world which retains its vault in anything like its entirety, and that is the small so-called Temple of Diana at Nimes. Unfortunately its shape is somewhat abnormal, as shown in the annexed plan. Hence, perhaps, its preservation, but it would be a more apt illustration if it had a peristyle instead of vaulted arches, but in consequence of this, the semicircular vault is nearly entire, and so is the great window by which it was lighted. Whether the dwarf portico below it, as represented in

Laborde's drawing, is quite correct, or whether it was protected by a portico of taller pillars, will only be known when it is looked at by some one who is

15.—Section of the Temple of Diana at Nîmes. (From Laborde.)

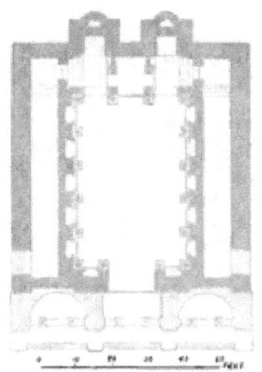

14. Plan of the Temple of Diana at Nîmes. (From Laborde.)

aware of the importance of this opening in the façade as a means of lighting the vault. From photographs I am inclined to believe in the correctness of Laborde's drawing. But whether there was a portico in front is of comparatively little importance. The great point of interest to us here lies in the great semicircular or rather segmental window by which light was introduced. It is also uncertain whether the balustrade shown in outline in the woodcut really existed. Even if it did, the opening is still more than sufficient to admit all the light that was required for a temple only 65 feet in depth and about 50 feet in width, and that it was introduced in the most pleasing manner can hardly be doubted by those who have ever seen the effect of this mode of lighting in the rock-cut temples of India.

The so-called Pretorium at Mousmieh is another example of the sort. It certainly was lighted by a great fanlight over the doorway, filling up the whole

[1] Laborde, Monuments de France, 1816. Revue Archéologique, June 16, 1877.

space inside the vault.[1] But it was not originally designed as a temple, though admirably adapted for the purpose if it had been so used. In this instance the window was originally segmental, following closely the line of the vault, which is 18 feet in span, while the doorway is only about 10 feet wide. Consequently, if made semicircular, the opening must have been brought so much lower down

— Portion of at Mousmieh. (From a Photograph.)

that part of the vault would have been imperfectly lighted—a defect that both here and at Nîmes the architects seem carefully to have avoided. They sought to admit the light at as high a point as possible, and in sufficient abundance at the highest point.[2] At Mousmieh the fanlight was protected by a portico of

---

[1] De Vogüé, Syrie Centrale, plate vii. p. 45. Neither the plate nor the woodcut shows the mode of lighting, but I possess photographs which do. The woodcut is taken from one of them.

[2] When the Christians converted this building into a church they built up the doorway and the segmental window over it, merely leaving a small opening for the door and four small windows to supply their place. They were thus content with between one-tenth and one-twentieth of the light that had been admitted by their Pagan predecessors. It is a strong proof how indispensable the ancients considered a flood of light to be for the illumination of their buildings, and how unlikely they were to be content with the expedients usually suggested for this purpose.

six pillars mounted on pedestals like those at Ephesus, with a very wide central intercolumniation protecting the doorway and window. My impression is that a similar portico existed at Nimes, though it is difficult to prove it. The date of this building, as ascertained from inscriptions, is about 180 A.D., which is certainly long subsequent to that at Nimes.

All the great Roman temples in Europe have been so completely ruined that there does not remain one which can be adduced as evidence either for or against the views here advocated, but at Baalbec in Syria there is one, which if properly examined would, I believe, be sufficient to settle the question.

No. Section of the Temple of Jupiter at Baalbec.
(Showing on the right, the section as represented by Wood and Dawkins, on the left, that proposed.)

Unfortunately no one has visited the place, since the publication of Wood and Dawkins's beautiful work in 1757, who either could observe correctly, or seems to have cared to do so.¹ Although the plates in their work are generally correct and stand the photographic test well, the canons of architectural criticism were not then well understood, and when closely examined the restorations are found to be extremely faulty. In the first place, looking at their section of the temple (Pl. XXXVI. and XL.), the vault is so high that if carried out with requisite thickness it would protrude through the line of the wooden roof, as shown by the pediments. At all events there is no room for

---

¹ In an article written by the late Sir Charles Barry for the Dictionary of Architecture, the various authorities are enumerated, and they are ludicrously discrepant, and he himself rather adds to the confusion he undertakes to clear up. Recently, M. Joyau, a French architect, a pupil of the Academy of Rome, visited the place and made a plan which surpasses all others in correctness, but so far as I can ascertain he made no elevation or restoration.

any properly formed wooden roof, and there is no sufficient abutment for the arch. It would not have stood for one hour after the centering was removed. It is curious that during the long time that has elapsed since the publication of their work (125 years) no one has observed this, but to any architect the impossi-

17.—HALF SECTION AND HALF ELEVATION OF THE TEMPLE AT BAALBEC.

bility of its being so constructed is obvious, and some means must have been taken by the original architects to obviate the difficulty. The defect will be understood by an examination of the section (woodcut 16), the right side of which is an exact copy of Wood and Dawkins's plate. On the left side my suggestion is represented, which at all events is a mechanical remedy, and, my impression is, a great artistic improvement. Nothing, to my mind, is so ugly and inartistic as the great flat roof of this, and indeed of most Roman temples, as represented in the plates of Wood and other works. Even if covered with tiles, as the roofs of Greek temples were, they must have been flat and unmeaning; and if with metal, which is much more probable, their insufficiency in an artistic sense must have been doubly apparent. On the other hand an attic, as I have introduced it here, would break up the flatness in a most satisfactory manner, and if the sloping parts of the roof, not occupied by the attic, were of the same stone, an architectural effect would be produced far more satisfactory than any yet attempted. The only difficulty is how to stop the attic at either end. At the west, as shown in the plan, woodcut 18, there is a division at about 50 feet from that end, and a screen across the temple inside, which seems to demand such an arrangement externally. About the same distance from the

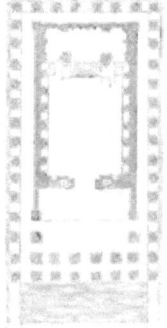

18.—PLAN OF TEMPLE AT BAALBEC.

east front—in spite of Vitruvius both the temples here enter from the east—the Turks have built a wall across the pronaos. If this wall were carried through the roof, it would answer perfectly to stop the attic. It is tolerably evident that this Turkish wall does replace a screen of some sort, for the cornices of the pronaos stop at it, and the masonry on the left hand between it and the true front of the temple is rough and unpolished to an extent not found in any other part of the temple. It would require that the foundation of the wall should be removed, and the whole floor of the pronaos examined in order to ascertain where the screen was placed, and how constructed, if indeed it can now be ascertained. But assuming it to be found, and its existence does not appear to me doubtful, the restoration of the temple appears to be easy. The pronaos had, in all probability, a flat ceiling in wood. There is no room, and no abutment for a vault. The vestibule had also a ceiling of wood covered with lead and drained to the right and left, and above this was a great semicircular window, as shown in the diagram, throwing a flood of light into the cella. This is no mere theory, for, if I mistake not, the curved stones that surrounded it are still to be seen in the photographs; the only difficulty is that no one who has yet visited these temples seems to have had eyes sufficiently educated to observe them.

There is another point with regard to the construction of this temple which requires explanation. On the slightest examination of the plan (in woodcut 18) it will be observed there are two stone staircases, one on either side of the entrance doorway, so commonly found in Greek temples. One at least of them is so perfect that it can be ascended at the present day. For what purpose were these stairs rather offensively obtruded into the cella at this point? If the end of the cella was a plain wall across the solid vault of the temple, as is generally supposed, these stairs are useless, and no attempt has yet been made by any one to explain why they were placed there. But the architects of this most beautiful of Roman temples were not likely to introduce such a feature without a motive. I cannot suggest any other than that a great window existed at the end of the temple, and that the management of its velia or shutters required easy access to it on the part of the servants of the temple.

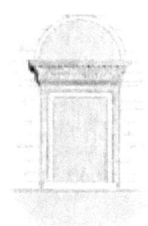

Arranged in this way the east front of the temple would take the form shown in the annexed woodcut, copied from the front of a building at Chaqqa,¹ which, with slight variations, may be said to be common at that age, and would hardly have been adopted unless these great semicircular windows over doors had been common at the time.

There is another illustration which may be quoted in favour of this view. In Captain Beechey's work on Cyrene² there is a view of a hexastyle temple, with an attic as large and as

---

¹ De Vogüé, Syrie Centrale, vol. i. pl. 2.
² Beechey's Explorations in North Africa, London, 1828.

important relatively as the one proposed for the Baalbec temple. As its value as an architectural illustration was not perceived by Captain Beechey, it is probably not quite correctly drawn, and, besides, is only a rock-cut model on a small scale, but, so far as I can judge, it could only have been executed if attics to temple-roofs were more common than we are in the habit of assuming. It is a thousand pities that when Messrs. Smith and Porcher visited the place, their attention was not directed to these rock-cut models. Cyrene, from its long-undisturbed state, seems to offer

20.—Rock-cut Tomb at Cyrene.
(From Capt. Beechey's Travels.)

numberless suggestions for the restoration of ancient buildings, but this requires that it should be visited by some educated architect, who has not only the knowledge requisite to observe, but the leisure to do so. This, unfortunately, has not yet been the case.

It would require many more illustrations, and text to a very much greater extent, to explain all the peculiarities of this beautiful temple of Baalbec; but it is hardly worth while to attempt to give them here. More can be done by an investigator on the spot in an hour than can possibly be effected in any time by any one unfamiliar with the locality, who must depend on plates published 120 years ago, and on photographs taken at random, for the sake of their picturesque, not their scientific value. Any traveller personally familiar with the temple, could easily rectify errors in detail which I may have fallen into from imperfect information, but I am not afraid that he will be able to controvert the main proposition that I have sought to establish. If I am not very much mistaken, the roof of this temple was formed with an attic, something like the one I have suggested, and the interior was lighted by a semicircular window above the great doorway; but how that was managed can only be determined by a careful examination of the masonry on the spot.

There is no difficulty in applying this system of lighting—which may be called the pseudo-hypæthral—to any of the great temples of Rome of which enough remains to enable us to understand their original arrangements. Unfortunately, the examples are few, and are made fewer by the architects being so possessed with the idea that the Romans roofed their temples by unroofing them, that they have not tried to find out how such arrangements as are now proposed could be fitted to the existing remains.

Fortunately there is one temple—or rather couple of temples—the remains of which are sufficiently entire for our purposes. The Temple of Venus and Rome, near the Colosseum, built by Hadrian, was the largest, and apparently the most beautiful temple of the capital; and, as if to give the lie to the assertion of Vitruvius, that all temples faced the west, this one consisted of two cellas, back to back, joined at the apses, one of which opened consequently to the east, the other to the west. Considerable difference of opinion exists, and always has existed, among antiquaries, as to the mode in which this temple should be restored. In Palladio's time, when naturally the ruins were more perfect than they are now, a peristyle was not dreamt of. He simply restored the two cellas back to back, and introduced a large triple window in the eastern and western walls, thus lighting them perfectly.[1] Since then, the platform on which the temples stand has been carefully examined, and frusta of columns, 6 feet 2 inches in diameter, have been found in the neighbourhood, which could hardly have belonged to any other temple. Considerable difficulty was experienced in fitting these data to the ascertained dimensions. If the columns were placed on the edge of the platform, the pseudo-dipteral arrangement resulted in an ambulatory 35 feet at least in width, which was evidently excessive, and even then the antæ could not be made

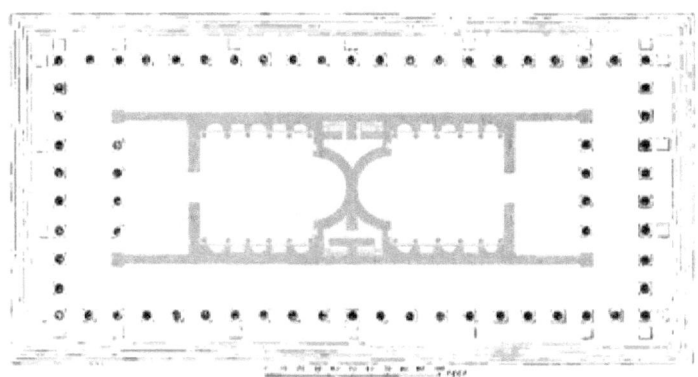

21.—PLAN OF THE TEMPLE OF VENUS AND ROME. (Restored by J. F.)

to fit with the third column of the porticoes. This difficulty was met by increasing the thickness of the walls by 7 or 8 feet, for which there is not only no authority, but it is absolutely contradicted by their appearance; and even then the space was left of 30 feet between the pillars and the walls.[2] A better solution of the difficulty seems to be afforded by the suggestion of a coin quoted by Canina,[3] which shows statues placed in front of the columns, as we may suppose they were at Ephesus, and with which Apollodorus, the architect of this temple, must have been familiar. Granting this—and of their existence there seems no reasonable doubt— we may reduce the platform by 10 feet at least all round, and so reduce the whole to harmony, as shown in the annexed woodcut, without any violence. Nothing

---

[1] Palladio, Architettura, lib. iv. ch. x.   Pardini, quoted by Donaldson, Numismata Arch.
[2] Canina, Arch. Romana, vol. ii. pls. lii. et seq.; p. 39.   [3] Canina, loc. cit. figs. 2 and 5.

remains of the pronaos of either temple, but we have only to borrow a hint from the temple at Baalbec, to fit it perfectly for the system proposed. In that temple the inner range of columns are shorter than those of the outer order by the whole height of the capitals. In this instance there seems no reason why it should not be even more, but, taking it as the same, it will be seen how perfectly it fits to the introduction of a semicircular window concentric with the vault, and how perfectly any sculpture that existed in the apse would be lighted by it. It may be a question whether the two hypæthra were or were not joined together by an attic externally, occupying the whole of the centre of the temple. My own impression is that this was the case. A long straight roof between the two tower-like forms would not be pleasing, but the attic, as at Baalbec, would, I believe, be a more pleasing variety to the usual monotony of Greek temple roofs. It would, besides, form an abutment to the vault which might be useful. I have not, however, represented it as continuous in the annexed woodcut, as it would require more

22.—HALF SECTION OF INTERIOR AND HALF ELEVATION OF TEMPLE OF VENUS AND ROME.

study to produce an agreeable form than I care at present to bestow upon it, and it involves more theory than the separate hypæthra shown in the drawing.

Comparing this temple with that of Jupiter Olympius, finished by the same emperor, we can observe several modifications in design that had taken place during the century and a half that elapsed since their main features were settled. Their dimensions are nearly exactly the same—175 feet by 362—but the Roman example is only pseudo-dipteral, instead of possessing the forest of columns of the temple at Athens. In some respect this may have been an improvement. There is a repose and a depth of shadow about a single range of columns standing at some distance from the wall, which may have been more effective than the crowded double range, though hardly sufficient to compensate for its magnificence. But the great change was the comparative shortness of the cellas, obviating the necessity of a complete hypæthron, with a window 50 feet in height, as in the Athenian example. In this—which may be called a pseudo-hypæthron—a semi-circular window, 25 feet in height, would more than suffice to light a cella only 80 feet in depth, and two temples could thus be accommodated with a peristyle that only sufficed for one in the other instance. Under these circumstances, I am inclined to think the pseudo-hypæthron a decided improvement on the full hypæthron. Externally, to the votaries approaching the temple, nothing interfered with the architectural ordinances, and all the mechanical arrangements were easy and perfect.

The great Temple of the Sun at Baalbec is also pseudo-dipteral, and shows the same tendency to shorten the cella as this Roman temple, though not to the same extent. It is decastyle and 163 feet wide, but with only nineteen columns in the flank, extending to 290 feet. The erection of a Christian Byzantine church, measuring 225 ft. by 120 ft., immediately in front of it, fully accounts for the disappearance of its cella, but so far as can be made out it appears to have been 160 feet in extent, supposing there was no opisthodomos, or any sanctuary behind the principal object of worship, which is very improbable. There probably was an apse or niche for the statue at nearly the same distance from the window as in the Temple of Venus and Rome.

The Temple of Mars Ultor at Rome, though only octastyle and 110 feet in width, is one of those short-cellaed temples which the Romans introduced, and which were certainly lighted in this manner. Though only 150 feet in depth, that is far too great a distance to be lighted by the door only, and nothing seems so easy as to introduce a window in the form suggested, and we may therefore fairly assume that the Romans did not neglect to do so, though most of the Roman temples have not been examined with sufficient care for us to ascertain exactly how it was effected.

It would be well, however, that this question should be more carefully investigated, because, in addition to the classes of temples just enumerated, there are a large class which almost certainly received their light through their doors only. The so-called Maison Carrée at Nimes, and the Temple of Jupiter in the Forum at Pompeii, are examples of this class with cellas 50 feet or less in depth, and with a large open pronaos in which most probably the altar stood, and where all the ceremonies of religion could be performed "coram populo." An image placed in the centre of a hall only 50 feet by 50 feet, would not require more light than it would receive from a doorway 8 feet by 12 feet. And many of the smaller Ionic temples were probably equally dependent on the doorway for the light they received, though, as above suggested, some of these may have had windows on each side of the doorway, which would be quite sufficient to light the interior when the doorway was closed.

On the other hand, the circular temples which did not admit, from their form, of windows of the class we have been describing, were lighted by windows of the class we now use, but to a greater extent than even we should think necessary. The Temple of Vesta at Rome, and of the Sybil at Tivoli,[1] have windows on each

---

[1] Isabelle, édifices circulaires, plates 6 and 7, 19 and 21.

side of the doorway, where one would think their introduction hardly necessary. The nine great windows of the Minerva Medica[1] are certainly in excess of the requirement according to our idea; they show how indispensable a flood of light was considered by the Romans.

At Palmyra, the great temple was lighted by four honest windows on each side, apparently because, being entered, from some cause, from the side, it was impossible to introduce an end light in the manner just described.[2] For utilitarian purposes the Palmyrene plan was probably quite equal to the other, but from an artistic point of view infinitely inferior.

It is hardly necessary to allude to the temples of Jupiter the Thunderer, of Fidius, and others, which Vitruvius mentions as hypæthral.[3] They were so in the sense that, like those of the god Terminus, they were placed in the open air, and were therefore in that sense hypæthral, ὕπαιθρος; but the word is here accidentally used with a totally different meaning from that it is intended to convey when applied to decastyle and dipteral temples of the first order.

Much need not be said in this place regarding the Pantheon at Rome, though it can hardly be passed over, as it is the *only temple* of the ancient world which has come down to our times which receives light from a hole in the roof, and as such has been so often quoted by those who advocate that mode of lighting.

The truth of the matter is, however, that the Pantheon was not originally erected as a temple at all. It was intended for the Laconicum of the Baths of Agrippa, and from the excavations recently carried out, in those of Caracalla, was as nearly as possible identical in size and in all its dispositions. It never, however, was apparently fitted up as a Chamber of the Baths, but, for some reason or other which we cannot now discover, was apparently, even in Agrippa's time, diverted from its original purpose before it was quite finished, and converted into a temple to " All the Gods."

Possibly this was done because it was, by an oversight of the architect, placed due north of the main building, and where the rays of the sun could never reach it, while in all the other Thermæ, as far as can now be ascertained, the laconicum faced the south-west, where it certainly would be exposed to the sunshine for the longest possible period. Whether this was the cause of the change or not, the transformation is certain. A portico was added on the north side, very beautiful in itself, but inferior to that of the Temple of Jupiter at Baalbec, but its effect painfully marred by its incongruity, and the clumsy manner in which it is fitted on to the rotunda.

---

[1] Isabelle, pls. 23 and 24.
[2] Wood and Dawkins, Palmyra, pls. xvi. xx.
[3] Vitruvius, book i. ch. ii. It is evident he did not consider these as hypæthral in the same sense as the decastyle temples which he enumerated under that designation when he said

" Hujus exemplar Romae non est." These small temples were all in Rome, and though the gods in them were exposed to the open air, their temples were not hypæthral in the sense in which Vitruvius understood the term.

[4] Virgil, Æn. ix. 445-8; Ovid, Fast. ii. 671.

As before remarked, the temptation was extremely great to use an opening in the centre of a dome to introduce light when wanted. Instead of being a source of weakness, as openings in the roof generally are, it was a source of strength—mechanically—and it was placed so high, 150 feet, that the heaviest shower would be resolved into spray before it reached the floor. Besides this, the very nature of its ritual form did not admit of a statue being placed in its centre under the eye of the dome, which might have been the case if it were dedicated to a single god. It apparently was to avoid this that it was dedicated to "All the Gods," and they were arranged in niches around the walls as in a Serapeon, where they were practically protected from atmospheric influences. Whether all this was so or not is of little consequence for our present purpose; there is at all events enough known of the history of the Pantheon and its original destination, to show that it was in every respect exceptional. No argument can consequently be derived from its original construction, or subsequent dedication, which can have the most remote bearing on the enquiry as to the mode in which light was introduced into temples which were erected originally for purposes of worship.

If this work were intended only as a disquisition on Greek and Roman temples it would be necessary to treat the subject in greater detail. It would require a far greater number of illustrations than are compatible with a work of this class to make this clear to those who have not studied the matter in detail. More than this, however, it is necessary that the remains of Roman temples should be studied with special reference to this theory before any definite conclusion can be arrived at. Many things are now omitted to which allusion would become indispensable, and some would require to be treated of at much greater length than has been thought appropriate in a work especially designed to illustrate the mode in which temples were lighted, and only incidentally how they were constructed. Enough, however, it is believed, has been said to show that, in introducing light into their temples, the Romans at least were wedded to no particular system. But the light of day was as essential to their temples as it is to our houses, and like true architects, they introduced it by any means they found most convenient, and at the same time most artistic. As a rule, they preferred lighting from the end, because the vaulted or semicircular form they adopted for the roofs of their temples rendered it not only more convenient but more appropriate. The Greek mode of lighting from the sides was, as we shall presently see, only adapted to horizontal roofs, and could not have been advantageously used with vaults. Hence the distinction between the two systems, though both were equally beautiful and appropriate as applied by the ancients. So perfect, indeed, do both systems appear, and so superior to any mode of lighting attempted in modern times, that it is difficult for those who have no experience of their effect to form an opinion regarding them. When the Greek mode has been described, we shall be in better position to judge between them. Though the two systems differed from each other in almost every essential particular, they were both so beautiful that he would be a bold man who would pronounce which was the best, without at least more experience than can easily be obtained in modern times.

All this will be clearer when we come to describe the mode in which Greek temples were lighted, but in the meanwhile it probably is not too much to repeat that, with the single exception of the Pantheon, there is no material evidence of any Roman temple being lighted by a hole in the roof. My own conviction is positive, for reasons stated above, that there is no passage in any ancient author which, if properly translated, would bear the interpretation affirming that such was the practice. It is true there is not much material evidence of the system here advocated, but there is some, and that of a very distinct character, but in addition to this, there seems the strongest possible probability in its favour. If the mode of lighting by counter-sunk windows in the roof in front of the apse, as I conceive was practised by the Romans, can be established, we have a mode introduced, which was not only mechanically perfect, but artistically most beautiful. If we are obliged to take refuge in the hole in the roof system, we are forced to admit that the Roman architects were incompetent bunglers who could not put a water-tight roof on their temples, and did not understand the first principles of æsthetic lighting.

I can have no hesitation which hypothesis to adopt, though it may require many more illustrations, and working it out with far more elaboration than is attempted here, before others feel so strongly as I do on the subject. But if the groundwork of the argument is sound, its elaboration may safely be left to those who can follow it up with greater advantages than are now available.

CHAPTER III.

ANCIENT GREEK TEMPLES.

In the preceding pages an attempt has been made to explain the motives that guided the Romans in introducing light into their temples, and the means they took for carrying out what they proposed in the most convenient and artistic manner. Whether I have or have not succeeded in explaining either theory in a satisfactory manner is not at the present time a matter that need concern us. The discussion has at least this advantage, which is really of importance for what is to follow; it enables us to approach the question as to how the Greeks introduced light into their temples, unencumbered with all those perplexing but irrelevant questions which have hitherto rendered the controversy one of the most obscure and unsatisfactory of any to be found in the whole range of architectural literature.

We are now fortunately able to define the age of the prevalence of the Grecian Doric order with very tolerable precision. We know of no temple that can be dated before the foundation of Syracuse in Sicily, in the 11th Olympiad (said to have been founded about B.C. 735[1]); and we know of none that were erected after the age of Alexander. If, therefore, we take 700 B.C. as the extreme date of the earliest temple, and 300 as the latest, we have four centuries to which the subjects of our enquiry are limited. Doric architecture, in fact, like every other form of Hellenic civilization, may be considered as having sprung into existence with the Olympiads, 776 B.C. All the art that is found in Greece before that time may safely be ascribed to a people whom, for want of a better name, we must be content to call Pelasgi. The culminating point of that ancient race was three or four centuries earlier. Between the two there is a gulph which we have at present no means of bridging over. There were, of course, temples, the precursors of the Doric, in Greece before 700; but it is only by inference that we can guess what their forms were, and it would be rash to call them Doric. So far as we can now see, their architecture was wholly of wood; and whether they assumed at that early age the forms which were afterwards characterized as Doric is more than we are at present able to decide. In like manner the Doric order was employed in secular buildings down to the time of the Roman Emperors, but it was a mere copying of the old and venerated form, without any

---

[1] Thucydides, vi. 2; Strabo, vi. 269.

special meaning, and with as little real purpose as when employed for churches in modern times.

This being so, it is evident that the Romans could have had no possible influence in the invention of the Grecian style, or its subsequent development. All their works are long posterior, and belong to a different development of art altogether. If, of course, we could trace any instance in which they copied directly any Greek form, it might aid us in understanding some obscure points in the controversy. But none such has been pointed out, nor am I aware of any single instance in which this has been done. There are indeed few things more remarkable in the whole history of architecture than to observe, at the time when Vitruvius wrote, how completely the Grecian Doric style had passed into the limbo of exploded and forgotten antiquities. The temples of Pæstum and Sicily must have been familiar to many Romans, but he never alludes to them, and it is questionable whether he ever mentions, except in the most incidental manner, those of Greece. Many passages which modern commentators have understood as applying to this order may more probably be applied to other and more modern examples.

When the Roman Cossutius, at an earlier age than most Roman temples, undertook to rebuild that of Jupiter Olympius, he did not even adopt the intermediate Ionic, but at once leapt to the favourite Roman Corinthian, as the only order worthy of notice, and all its features were moulded in that crucible. It has been hinted above that it is possible the Roman Doric may have had another origin than in the Grecian order bearing that name; but whether that was so or not, nothing is more striking than the utter contempt the Romans felt for the order we so fervently admire; and consequently nothing is more clear than that, as they did not aid in its development, neither did they contribute to or perpetuate any of its forms or features. Though it is, of course, difficult to prove a negative, the fair inference from all this is that the Roman mode of introducing light to their temples probably differed essentially from that employed by the Greeks; and certainly, in so far as any material evidence is concerned, there is none to show that the Romans in any instance used an opaion or clerestory, which, as we shall presently see, was the mode universally used in Greek temples.

The fact of the matter is, that Egypt is the only country in the ancient world which, either from its geographical position or its ancient history, could have contributed anything towards the development of the Grecian style, or have given her any hints as to the mode of lighting her temples. Yet, strange to say, Egypt is the only country that has hardly ever been alluded to in these hypæthral controversies. This is the more remarkable as it is now generally admitted that there existed in Egypt a Proto-Doric style, at least a thousand years before the known existence of any example in Greece, and that the Egyptian Proto-Doric style had the most essential influence on the subsequent development of the Grecian order. In like manner it is nearly certain—I think quite so—that the mode in which the hypostyle temple at Karnac was lighted was the type which the Greeks long sought to imitate, and, at least a thousand years afterwards, succeeded in carrying out at Eleusis and still more successfully in the glorious clerestory of the Parthenon. This was accomplished not by direct copying, it is true, but it was indirectly developed in the manner which it is the object of the following pages to explain.

It now only remains to try and realize a distinct idea of the state of the arts in Greece at the time the Doric order was introduced or invented, in order to enable us to approach the question that now occupies us, unembarrassed by any extraneous considerations. So soon, however, as we attempt to look closely into this question, we become aware of some most unexpected results that arise in connexion with this question. Greece was inhabited before the time of the Dorians, or Hellenes as they are generally known, by a highly civilized race, practising all the arts of life in a very perfect form, but their civilization was totally different from that which succeeded it. It may indeed be said to be antagonistic to the succeeding forms, which disappeared on the introduction of the Hellenic races, and their arts hardly left any trace of their prior existence in those of the people that followed them.

When first I wrote on this subject, I was careful to distinguish between what I have called the Pelasgic form of arts and those of the Hellenes who succeeded them. The former I assumed commenced with the foundation of Argos, said to be about 1800 B.C., and ceased to exist with the return of the Heraclidæ eighty years after the war of Troy;[1] and from that chronology and ethnography I have since seen no reason to swerve. Since then, however, much that was then vague and undetermined has acquired strength and precision, from the researches and discoveries of Schliemann at Mycenae and Orchomenos. At the last-named place he discovered a beautifully ornamented roof to the thalamus, or inner chamber, which is no doubt coeval with the erection of the main building,[2] and which settles for ever the age of the gold and bronze ornament he had previously discovered in Mycenae. The tomb-stones there, the gold ornaments,[3] and, generally, the whole character of the art, is absolutely identical. There can thus be no doubt that all belong to the same age. We have, therefore, the two great treasuries, tombhouses of Atreus and Minyas, built with great skill, and employing large—it may be said, gigantic—masses, and several smaller treasuries, showing the same perfection of masonic art. We know that they were ornamented, and covered internally with plates and ornaments of bronze. These, it is true, have all perished, and we cannot quite realize their forms, except that from the contem-

---

[1] True Principles of Beauty in Art, 1849, p. 329.
[2] Orchomenos Ausgrabungen, von Dr. H. Schliemann, Leipzig, 1881. Journal Hellenic Studies, vol. ii. p. 1.
[3] Schliemann's Mycenae, figs. 140, 144, 145 for tomb-stones, 344, 366, 472, 476 for gold ornaments, and for the double honeysuckle 151.

porary gold work in the adjacent tombs we may gather that it was characterized with the elegance that belongs to all their works in metal. But with all this civilization and knowledge of the arts, it is rather startling to find that they had no knowledge of letters—at least not a scrap of any inscription has been found—and no coins. But what is of more importance for our present purpose, no knowledge of iron; not even the stain of rust has been found anywhere, and this must easily have been detected even if the metal itself had perished.

Who then were this people who occupied, so far as we know, the whole of Greece before the Dorian invasion? The term Pelasgi, which is usually applied to them, conveys no distinct ethnographic meaning, though for that very reason, at present at least, convenient. Of their language we know nothing, but, if we may trust Herodotus,[1] it was something very different from the Greek in which he wrote, but he affords us no clue to its connexion with other tongues.[2] The one mode, therefore, of tracing their affinities is by their architecture; and till the science of Architectural Ethnography is more appreciated and better understood than it is in this country, this is hardly available for elucidating this question.

As far as we can at present see, all their affinities were with the Phrygians on the one hand and the Etruscans on the other. They had no temples properly so called, but tombs innumerable. Their worship was of the Manes of their ancestors, and their deities belonged almost exclusively to the infernal regions. Unlike the æsthetic and joyous religion of the Dorians who succeeded them, theirs was a gloomy ancestral worship which may have had affinities with that of Egypt, though we can trace very few similarities with it in the architecture of that country. But the point that interests us most here is the knowledge that their architecture had no influence whatever on the Doric style. It may have had on the Ionic, and probably had, though we hardly know how to understand the term as applied to a style in that early age. When for instance Pausanias talks of the brazen treasury of Myron at Olympia, one of the apartments of which was adorned in the Ionic, the other in the Doric style,[3] we feel that the distinction was then (648 B.C.) understood, but how expressed it is difficult to understand.[4] There were apparently no pillars in the treasury, and it must have been that some sort of flowing spiral was the characteristic of the Ionic style, as it was of the Pelasgic, and some kind of square fret had been invented and applied by the Dorians. At least we find that in all the

---

[1] Herodotus, i. 57.

[2] It is by no means clear that those who warred at Troy could speak a word of Greek, as we now know that language. They were Phrygians on the one side and Pelasgi on the other, and neither of these people certainly spoke any language at all like the classical Greek of the great age.

[3] Pausanias, Book vi. ch. xix. p. 497.

[4] The treasury of Myron has not been identified by the Germans among the numerous others which they uncovered there. My own impression is that it is still buried in what appeared to them as a spur of Mount Kronos, but which, as shown in woodcut No. 48, seems very like the exterior of a treasury. When their final work is published all this will no doubt be explained.

subsequent stages of Greek art the flowing spiral as distinguished from the angular square was a principal form of these two branches of art, and may very early have been their leading characteristic.

Except for this reminiscence, the Pelasgic style disappeared from Greece absolutely, with the so-called return of the Heraclidæ. There was no war of extermination, no massacre of the people, but apparently only the gradual supersession of a weaker race by a stronger one. But even in an inferior position there is no reason to suppose that their arts perished with their supremacy. The building experiences which they had gained remained the property of their successors. Their skill in working in gold was not lost, and above all their proficiency in casting and carving bronze became the metal art of all Europe, and a great part of Asia, till long afterwards. Eventually it was superseded by the introduction of the cheaper but more useful iron, which now has everywhere supplanted the more artistic compound of copper with tin or zinc.

The religion which the Dorians introduced and practised was as complete a contrast as can be imagined to the gloomy superstition of the Pelasgi. Their gods dwelt in Olympus, fed on ambrosia, and drank nothing but the delicious nectar. They were mortals in their form and passions, and also it must be confessed in their frailties, but greater than mortals in their beauty and by their immortality. The task, therefore, that the Dorians set to their architects was to provide for their gods abodes larger and more beautiful than the dwellings of men; to their sculptors to represent these gods, as mortals but more dignified, and in all respects so perfect as to distinguish them from their sublunar prototypes. To the painter they assigned the task of heightening the effects the architect had sought to produce, and of completing the story as told by the sculptor by introducing figures and effects beyond the compass of his art; while the jeweller and worker in metal, with the most exquisite detail, added the preciousness which sufficed to elevate the image of the god beyond all comparison with mortal men. No religion ever offered so many inducements and so many opportunities for the full development of the arts in all their glory, and we should not, therefore, feel surprised if after two centuries spent in trying to perfect the Greek peripteral temple, they at last produced in the Parthenon the completest development of all that we know of that was beautiful and grand.

It need hardly be suggested that for the four or five centuries, during which the Dorian Greeks were acquiring supremacy in Greece, they must have had temples of some sort in which to shelter the images of their gods and themselves while worshipping them. These probably were small, and built with perishable materials, but it is somewhat singular that all have perished, and not one material trace of any one is anywhere to be found.[1] Even if we take the institution of the

---

[1] There is a small temple or cell in the 'Carystos,' which was first noticed by Walpole island of Eubœa on the mountain of Ocha, near | (Travels in Greece, p. 288, pl. not numbered).

Olympian games as the earliest period at which we might expect the Greeks to be building temples of any permanent character, we have still a long interval to pass over before we find any remains of any of them to which we can affix anything like a certain date. Under these circumstances it is fortunate that Greeks, like most other nations, when they undertook to translate their primæval wooden architecture into stone, did it so literally that we are generally able to recognize the original wooden form in stone, and thus, to a certain extent at least, supply the deficiency.

who gives two plates illustrating it. In so far as the front elevation is concerned they are the best yet published, but his diagrams of the roof, which principally interests us, are quite unintelligible, which is strange, as he was assisted by an architect, Mr., afterwards Sir Robert, Smirke, who ought to have known better. Afterwards it was more fully illustrated by M. Ulrichs in the publications of the Archæological Society of Rome (Ann. dell' Inst. Archæo., vol. xiv. 1842, p. 6, plate xxxvii.), and has been frequently quoted as an instance in point by those who advocate the hole in the roof theory. Unfortunately, Herr Ulrichs, though a very learned man and a good draughtsman, was no architect, and did not in the least comprehend the constructive peculiarities of the building he was describing, and it is impossible from either his or Sir R. Smirke's drawings to make out how the roof was formed.

The building is of undoubted Pelasgic masonry, measuring 42 feet by 25 externally, and 32 by 16 internally, and is roofed by four or five courses of stones overlapping one another, and each projecting slightly beyond the stone beneath it, but without their edges being bevelled off, as is the case generally in the "Treasuries" and other buildings of the Pelasgic age. In this instance they were only employed as a system of bracketing to support the external roofing slabs.

Only one of the external roofing stones remains *in situ*. It is situated over the doorway and measures 14 feet in length by 6 feet 6 inches in width, and though we have no section showing the angle of the roof, it is evident these roofing stones were not long enough to meet in the centre. In fact, even with the most perfect masonry—this is not—it is evident that two stones meeting at the centre is a very bad mode of forming a ridge, which, so far as I know, was never practised anywhere by any people. In this instance a gap is left 20 inches wide by 20 feet in length, through which the sunshine, to say nothing of the rain

and snow in that climate, must have most seriously inconvenienced the worshippers. A ridge piece, either flat, along the dotted line of woodcut No. 23, or better in an inverted V shape, as shown in the annexed woodcut, is indispensable, and no doubt existed here, but having been removed, as almost all of the external roofing stones have been, has given rise to the hypæthral theory.

23.—DIAGRAM EXPLANATORY OF SUGGESTED RIDGE PIECE OF TEMPLE AT OQUA.

If the builder of this temple really left this long hole in the roof, it could only have been for the purpose of admitting the snow and rain. It certainly was not for the sake of admitting light to the interior. There are two windows existing in the external wall, one on each side of the doorway amply sufficient in that climate to admit all the illumination required. Even assuming that they are too small, they could easily have been increased to any extent—equal in fact to the doorway for this purpose. It seems to me impossible to believe that having two windows and a doorway amply sufficient to admit any amount of light, the masons even if Pelasgi would have recourse to so clumsy an expedient as half unroofing their temple for such a purpose. All theories based on the stupidity and consequent inaptitude of Greek architects—even if Pelasgi—seem to me to rest on a very insufficient basis, and would require much clearer evidence than is afforded by this temple before they can be admitted.

From all subsequent experience we gather that the formative idea of the original Greek temple was a square or oblong hall to contain the image, preceded by a porch of equal or nearly equal extent to protect the doorway. This porch was apparently always formed by continuing the walls of the hall or cella to the required extent, and terminating them in what were called *antæ*, or *parastads*, between which two pillars were inserted. The use of the latter is not immediately apparent. The same truss or framing that carried the roof of the cella could equally well carry that of the porch, and as there is no trace of pillars being used in the cellas of primitive temples, there seems at first sight no reason for their being used in the porch. It must, however, be borne in mind that the roof decoration, resting on the side walls, was necessarily carried across the porch where the same support was not available, and besides, in an architectural sense, a gaping portal without any subdivision would have been intolerable.

My own impression is, that these original pillars were simply squared posts, without any diminution towards the base or capital. There is no mechanical reason why a wooden support should swell anywhere except in the centre; its strength is the same throughout, and the best carpentry form is that of a beam with its supports let into the foundation on which it rests. When so used it is mechanically perfect. We have, however, no example of this. In the celebrated "François vase" there is a little portico in antis over a fountain which lets us into

a secret we should not otherwise be aware of.[1] It seems the Greeks in a very early age used a bracket capital, which we should certainly expect they would, in a purely carpentering age, but all trace of this is lost in the earliest examples that remain to us. Even in the age when the vase was painted (about 500 B.C.), we see the influence of stone architecture in the tapering form of the supports; and in the corresponding temple on the same vase we have a Doric temple in antis,

---

[1] Monuments inédits de l'Institut Archéologique, vol. vi. pl. liv., lviii.

very literally rendered, and with the pillars sloping inward, and the stone capitals complete. Though, therefore, we may assume the bracket capitals of the example to be the reminiscence of a very early form, it only proves that this capital continued to be used in secular erections long after it had been superseded by a different form borrowed from stone architecture in sacred buildings. As it is in vain to hope that any remains of these ancient astylar temples will now be found in Greece, it only remains to us to try and recover their primitive forms from the copies of them in stone found in the perfected architecture of the country. For this purpose we cannot do better than select the Parthenon as an example, though as being the most perfect in existence it is perhaps furthest removed from the wooden original; but it is the best known and the best illustrated of any, so that we are not likely to fall into any mistakes in relying on its forms.

20.—Angle of the Parthenon.
(From Penrose's True Principles of Athenian Architecture.)

As will be seen from the annexed woodcut, the most marked and peculiar constructive feature in the whole composition is the triglyph. It is unlike anything else used in architecture, but so essentially was it considered a feature belonging to the Doric, that it was always used even by the Romans, though they admitted its inconvenience, and the difficulty at times of accommodating it to their designs.¹ It has been suggested—which, indeed, is obvious enough—that it represents the end of one of the beams of the roof; but no one, so far as is known, has yet attempted to explain why it was triple—a triglyph, in short. Yet the explanation seems simple enough. What the Greeks wanted was a form of roofing-truss which would be strong and light, not involving any complicated carpentry form, and above all, that could be constructed without the use of iron or other metal, which in the early ages of Greece was rare, and consequently expensive. In order to understand the mode in which the Greeks set about constructing this, it is only necessary to assume that at an early age they had learned to form timber into planks of varying thicknesses. Whether this was done with saws or other tools can hardly now be determined. My own impression is that saws were used at a very early age. The Greeks themselves ascribed their invention to Daedalus, which merely means that they had no certain knowledge on the subject; but the Egyptians used them at a very early period, as we know from their paintings, but how early it is impossible to say. Besides, it is very unlikely that so civilized a people as the Pelasgi certainly were, and using timber to such an extent as they certainly did in their houses and ships, should not eagerly have adopted, and perhaps perfected, so useful an invention. Certain it is that the ships in which the Pelasgic warriors sailed to the conquest of Troy were not mere "dug-outs." They were formed of planks, and most probably fastened to ribs by wooden trenails, as has been the universal practice in wooden shipbuilding down to the present day. But the real proof, in so far as the present argument is concerned, is that all the stone roofs we now know were copied from wooden prototypes which were built up of planks of various thicknesses, however formed. It is therefore a "question oisive" for our present purpose to try and ascertain how this was done. There is no instance of simulated log construction anywhere, or anything that would lead us to suppose that mere squared timbers were used, in any parts of their primitive temples.

That the Greeks had unlimited supplies of timber eminently suited for the purposes of roofing is certain. Probably the best were the cedars and pines of the Olympian range, or the mountains above Parnassus, which could easily be split into planks, and afterwards smoothed by adzes and other planing tools into planks of any required shape and thickness. But however it was effected, it certainly does not seem asking too much to assume that, at a very early age, a people so civilized as the Pelasgi, and after them the Dorians, found means of cutting these timbers into planks suitable for the roofing of their temples.

Assuming this, therefore, the annexed diagram, based on what we find in the Parthenon, as shown in the last woodcut, represents with very tolerable certainty the form of roofing adopted for a hall or cella of about 20 feet span. The centre timber or tie-beam I assume to have been 3 inches thick by 1 foot in

¹ Vitruvius, lib. iv. ch. 3.

breadth. On each side of this were placed two planks of the same thickness, meeting at the centre at the low angle always adopted by the Greeks as sufficient in their country to throw off the rain. On the tie-beam stood a king post, which was inserted between the lateral rafters, and so served to secure their junction, and it supported the tie-beam itself by a fashion-piece of corresponding thickness to the lateral rafters. Two struts seem to have been necessary in addition to these parts to steady the lateral rafters, and to combine the whole solidly together. No notches or other carpentry fitting or framing was required. The whole was formed by simple planks cut off only at the ends, according to the use to which

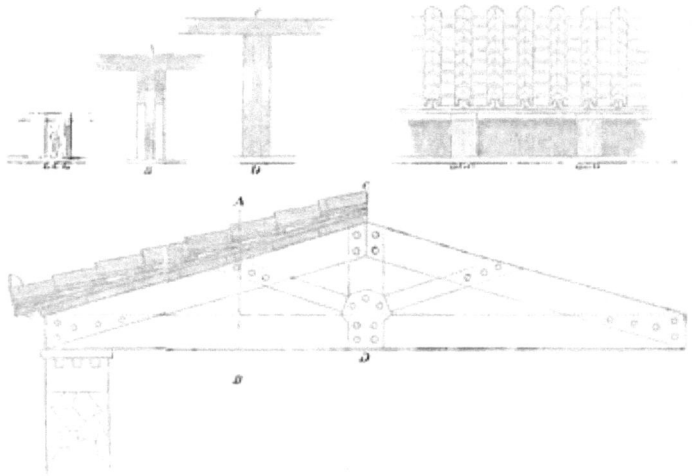

27.—Diagram explanatory of the mode in which the primitive roofs of Greek temples were formed.

they were to be employed. The whole were fastened together by wooden tre-nails, which were the best possible means of effecting that purpose. These were probably driven in tight, as is now the fashion in wooden shipbuilding; but they would have made a framing nearly equally strong, though not quite so, if used as movable pins. This seems to have been the mode, according to Pliny, in which they were used in the roof of the Buleuterion of Cyzicus, where the roof was constructed " without iron," in such a manner that it could be taken to pieces and stowed away, when not required.[1] This evidently could easily be done with such a roof as that shown in the diagram.

[1] Pliny, xxxvi. ch. 15.

The principal point of interest, however, to us at present is that the arrangement led irresistibly to the formation of the triglyph. Even if the ends of the three timbers were sawn off even, the triple arrangement would have been visible; but like true artists, the Greeks bevelled off the angles of the planks, so as to accentuate the construction, and make it what we now find. In the example in the diagram we are now describing, the triglyph would have been about 9 inches broad by rather more than a foot in height, which is about the proportion it generally afterwards retained.

In the diagram I have represented, the roof-trusses are placed about 3 feet apart, not only because the construction seems to require it, but because it affords a metope sufficiently large to light the interior. A range of metopes, 1 foot high by 3 feet wide, running round three sides of the cella, with the doorway in the front, would in that climate be sufficient to light the cella brilliantly, and all the openings would be sufficiently protected from the weather by the portico or the eaves, and the light introduced at the most pleasing angle, and without the direct rays of the sun being ever able to penetrate to the interior. It is indeed such an arrangement as we might expect from a Greek architect, and may therefore be accepted without hesitation.

The roof frames were, I conceive, held in their places by planks, placed either closely together, or slightly apart, so as to form a uniform ceiling, uninterrupted by purlins or any complicated carpentry forms of the sort. Had any such existed, they must inevitably have appeared in the architecture of the pediments, where, however, there is no trace of them.

In this system these ceiling planks were crossed at right angles with others running from the ridge to the eaves, on which the tiles rested, and may consequently be called the roofing planks. According to the example of the Parthenon, these were not placed touching one another as the ceiling planks, but with an interval between them, probably arising from some mode of fixing the tiles which we do not now quite understand. But the last tile required to be propped up by a fashion-piece extending along the whole front, in order that it might have the same slope as the others. It did not, of course, require 18 trenails to keep this in its place, any more than it required 6 guttæ to represent the pins that fastened down the wall plate to the stone; but in both these instances it was thought necessary to exaggerate the concealed construction in external ornament. In like manner the actual thickness of the roof was exaggerated in the Parthenon example in a manner not easily accounted for, apparently to give it the solidity necessary for stone construction.[1]

[1] Since the above was in type I have received from Herr Dörpfeld, through Dr. Schliemann, a drawing of which the annexed woodcut is a facsimile. It represents a form of roof which he worked out from an inscription, describing the "ship arsenal of Philon," and is extremely interesting as supplying some facts which were otherwise puzzling, and others which are entirely new. When Herr Dörpfeld publishes the inscription with a translation and diagrams, which

It seems needless to enlarge more upon this subject, for the present at least. Enough has probably been said to show that as a decoration the upper part of the Doric order is only a copy in stone of the wooden forms used in earlier temples, the details of which every one can work out for himself. Even if there is some discrepancy of opinion about particular features, there can, I fancy, be no doubt about the main proposition.

As a matter of construction, it appears that the roofing truss, as explained in the last diagram, is simply perfect. At least I feel certain that no truss has been invented or used in modern times in which the same amount of timber has been so scientifically arranged to obtain the utmost possible strength combined with the utmost simplicity of construction, and without the necessity of using iron or any other metal in its formation. The very perfection with which it fulfils all the conditions to which it was employed is in itself sufficient proof that it was invented by Greeks for Grecian purposes, and till something better is invented we may safely assume that it was employed by them in the early temples.¹

When, however, we descend below the tenia, or wall plate on which this framework of the roof rested, we become aware of a totally different class of

I have no doubt he will do, we shall be in a better position to speak about it. Meanwhile, however, the points that interest us most here are the separation from each other of the roof planks by an interval of about 3 inches, which accounts for the interval between the mutules of the Parthenon which was otherwise inexplicable. The smaller plank laid on these spaces would both constructively and artistically be an improvement.

The layer of clay, or concrete, between the planks of the roof and the tiles is quite new and

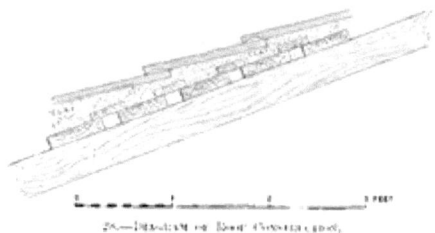

not before expected, but now that it is pointed out it may be accepted as explaining the thickness of the upper member of the Parthenon cornice, which, before I received these drawings, appeared to me anomalous." Altogether the drawing is most ingenious and entirely satisfactory, either as confirming the suggestions already made or suggesting new features in confirmation of the system adopted in this work.

¹ If iron had not so completely superseded wood in the construction of roofs I believe a patent for this form of Greek triglyphal truss would be valuable. It might be used with considerable advantage in modern building.

* I don't know whether Herr Dörpfeld has seen my scheme of roofing Greek temples, as published in the Builder of April [?], but I sent a copy at the time to my friend, Dr. Schliemann at Athens. He may have seen it there.

suggestions. In the first place, we have an architrave of great simplicity of form and great proportional strength, but this becomes appropriate as representing the wall on which the roof originally rested; below this again we have an order of pillars which, like the architrave, have not a single wooden suggestion about them. As before remarked, there is no constructive reason why a wooden post should taper upwards. The one thing to guard against mechanically is torsion, and for that reason it ought to be thicker in the middle; but the true mechanical form is a log of the same thickness throughout. If the Greeks ever used unhewn trunks of trees in their temples, there might be some ground for the suggestion, but there is no trace of them anywhere, and a people who could form so perfect a roofing truss as that just described were very far past the age for employing unhewn trunks as the pillars to support their roofs. Besides this, the abacus and echinus are quite antagonistic to wooden construction. If carpentry was ever used, it must have been in some manner like that suggested by the François vase (woodcut, No. 24). The wooden pillars must have been framed into the wooden architrave by some sort of bracket capital, and the whole depended for stability on framing, not on gravity, which is the essential characteristic of the Doric order as we now know it.

As it seems, therefore, clear that the Greeks did not evolve the Doric pillar out of any form they had previously used, we are forced to the only alternative that seems open to us, that they borrowed it from some previously existing style

29.—Façade of Tomb at Beni Hassan.
(From a sketch by Sir Charles Barry.)

elsewhere. In this case we have not far to go to find the original; for at Beni Hassan, in the Nile valley, we have a series of tombs of the twelfth dynasty, consequently at least a thousand years before any example found in Greece. The façades of these are adorned with a Proto-Doric order, very similar to that found afterwards in Greece. The pillar and architrave are nearly identical, but above that, as might be expected, we do not find any of those parts which represent the roof in the Doric. These tombs were roofed with simulated flat segmental arches, constructed probably with mud bricks, and all that was therefore wanted was a slight flat thatch of reeds to protect them from the rain, which was a rare occurrence in that country. In Egypt, where they always used stone for building purposes, we can trace these pillars from the form of a square prism fitted to a square architrave, and then canted off till we come to a polygon of 24 or 32 faces. When the latter is the case, an abacus becomes almost indispensable to fit the two together, and seems always to have been used; but the echinus is an invention the origin of which does not seem so clear. The meeting, however, of the perpendicular lines of the shaft with the horizontal lines of the abacus must always have seemed sharp and abrupt, and it must have been felt even by the Egyptians—who were not sentimental architects—and certainly by the Greeks, that the interposition of some moulding was requisite to get over the harshness of the contrast. It was not, however, generally employed in Egypt, though a capital of the 18th dynasty, found and figured by Falkener, is perhaps sufficient to prove that it was sometimes used as shown in the annexed woodcut.[1]

30.—ANCIENT CAPITAL FROM THE SACRED TEMPLE AT KARNAC. (Drawn by Ed. Falkener.)

It thus happens that the Proto-Doric, as used at Beni Hassan, is the exact complement of the Græco-Doric order, but does not overlap it in any part. The pillar, the massive architrave, and the flat vault, representing the stone lacunaria, are all copied from the Egyptian, and are easily traced back to their origin in that country.[2] But there is no suggestion there of the sloping roofs and timber framings of the Grecian temples. The covering of reeds is suggested at Beni Hassan, but it is omitted in Grecian art, to be replaced by their timber construction, so that there is now no feature of the Grecian Doric order, which cannot be explained by what is added, or what is omitted from these two examples in Egypt or at Athens.

If this were the proper place to do so, it would be easy and profitable to extend these remarks to a much greater length, but enough has probably been said to prove that we may now almost certainly assert that the Doric pillar, with its abacus, was a development of stone architecture, and borrowed from the Egyptian, most probably with the echinus, but that is not so clear. The architrave was common to both styles, but as used by the Greeks it may have been an original invention of theirs, without any hint from foreign sources. The triglyph, the metope, the cornice, and all the forms of the roof, were adopted by the Greeks, from their primitive wooden architecture, and are wholly original and their own.

The only temple now known to exist in Greece which has the least claim to be classed among the pre-hellenic examples, is that of Themis at Rhamnus.[3] Its walls are of Cyclopean or Pelasgic masonry, and it may originally have had a wooden roof, and been lighted by metopes. But if this were so, it has been completely remodelled in modern times. The antæ, with the pillars between them and the entablatures, are all of the perfected style, and show no trace of the primitive arrangement. In like manner, though the Temple of Diana Propylæa[4]

---

[1] An attempt has been made to discredit this discovery of Falkener's, but plate 83 of the first part of Leipsius's great work is sufficient to vindicate his accuracy. It is there, indeed, represented as a base, but the quoted diameters of the two fragments, 98 centimetres and 103, are sufficient to contradict the ascription.

[2] Antiquities of Ionia, vol. iv., Introd. p. 3.
[3] Antiquities of Attica, chap. vii. pl. 1 to 5.
[4] Id. chap. v. pl. 1 to 8.

at Eleusis is in plan a copy of an ancient amphiprostyle temple, without a peristyle, and could consequently have been easily lighted through the metopes, there is no means of ascertaining now, whether this was done or not. It is too completely ruined, but what remains is so essentially of the completely perfected style that it is probable that the only light was introduced through the doorway. At least we know that at this time Ionic temples were so treated. The little temple of Nike Apteros certainly received no light but through the front wall, but though the cella was barely 15 feet square, so studious were the architects that the lighting should be sufficient, that they cut away the whole of the wall on each side of the doorway, leaving only two narrow square pilasters to mark its place. There is, so far as I know, no architectural building in modern times, even when plate-glass is available, which is so completely lighted as this, though there is nothing about it that is otherwise exceptional. When its cella was so perfectly lighted, it seems impossible to contend that others were not so, as completely as their artistic exigencies required, provided the constructive difficulties

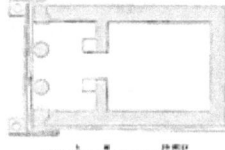
51.—Temple of Themis at Rhamnus.

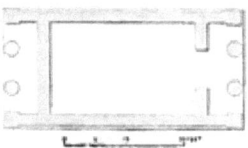
52.—Diana Propylæa, Eleusis.

could be overcome, which we hope presently to show could easily be accomplished. In like manner the little temple on the Ilissus[1] was certainly only lighted from the front, but as its cella was again only about 15 feet square, a doorway 6½ feet wide, with or without a window on each side, was amply sufficient for the purpose. There are Ionic temples, however, which never had or could have pretended to have any kind of metopal lighting; but the Greeks, having been accustomed in the great age to a class of small temples lighted only from the front, may have adopted the same form in small Doric temples of the same class, without reference to their primordial forms. We cannot, however, feel certain of this; and unless some remains are found, tending either to confirm or refute this view, the question must, for the present at least, remain in abeyance, and is likely to do so for some time. These old astylar temples of the Greeks were so small and so insignificant that it is hardly likely any examples still remain unappropriated to other purposes, or not utilized by the villagers in the localities in which they were situated.

---

[1] Stuart's Antiquities of Athens, chap. ii. pls. 1 to 8.

To the antiquary it would, of course, be extremely interesting to find a cella lighted through the metopes; but to the architect it is of singularly little importance, in consequence of an invention, or innovation, that took place at a very early age, which revolutionized the whole system of Greek temple architecture, and gave it that new form which it ever afterwards retained. We shall probably never be able to ascertain exactly, in what parts and to what extent it was an entire novelty, but the general result was something very different from the primæval form we have hitherto been describing. This was caused by the introduction of two more pillars in the portico of the front and rear of the temple, and a range of twelve or thirteen pillars on its flanks—thus giving rise to the hexastyle peripteral temple, which the Greeks adopted at once when it was first introduced to their notice, and from which they hardly ever swerved during the great age.

After this form was introduced it was so universally employed, that one of the principal reproaches which casual observers have to make to Greek architecture is its monotony. To the superficial student, it is true, all Greek temples seem very much alike, but when studied as they deserve to be, it is found that they contain as much variety of design, especially in their interiors, as is compatible with the canons of true taste. One of the objects of this work is to attempt to illustrate this, to some extent at least.

CHAPTER IV.

GREEK PERISTYLAR TEMPLES.

From the extreme simplicity of their parts, it is evident that these early temples of the Greeks—distyle in antis—were incapable of any great increase of magnificence except by magnifying their size at the great risk of making them vulgar and unmeaning. Even by adding a free standing portico of four columns in front and a like portico in the rear—introducing, in fact, what is called the prostyle and amphiprostyle plans—this did not add much to the splendour of the temple, and apparently was never adopted by the architects in Doric temples, though common enough in those erected with the Ionic order. When, however, the peristylar arrangement was suggested, as shown in the annexed woodcut, it

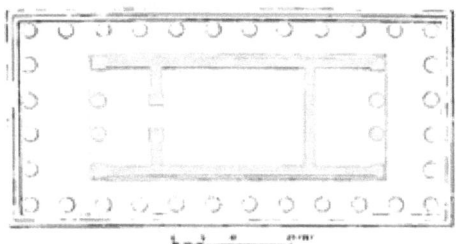

52.—Temple of Nemesis, Rhamnus.

was regarded at once as a solution of the difficulty. It was adopted at once, and everywhere, and persevered in with a persistency hardly known elsewhere in the history of art. After its invention all peristylar temples were built on this plan, with two striking exceptions²—the great temple at Selinus, and the Parthenon, which were octastyle. All the others had six columns in front and rear, and only varied in the number of those in the flanks. Sometimes there were as few as twelve, and in one instance at least, in a temple at Selinus, as many as seventeen.

Who then was the author of this suggestion? Curiously enough, we have no hint in any work that has come down to us who built the first peristylar temple. No name is, even traditionally, attached to this capital improvement, which revolutionized the style. When the books were written which we now

---

¹ Antiquities of Attica, chap. vi. pls. 1 to 13. It is doubtful whether the enneastyle at Pæstum should be considered as a temple or a forum.

possess, the form was looked upon as primæval, and no one thought it necessary to enquire how it arose. No other was known, or, it was assumed, could ever have existed.

When we come to enquire where it was first introduced, we are equally at fault. According to present appearances, with our present knowledge, the earliest examples are found at Ortygia in Sicily, and Metapontum in Magna Græcia.[1] But it is so extremely improbable that these provincial examples were the earliest, that we must pause for further information before assuming that they were the first. Hitherto it has been generally assumed that the temple at Corinth was the earliest known example, and it may be so in so far as the continent of Greece is concerned, but with the knowledge we now have, we are enabled to say, from the form of the echinus and the shape of the pillars, that it is not earlier than 600 B.C., and some of the provincial examples are certainly older than this. How much earlier, it is at present impossible even to make a plausible guess. But as it is convenient, for the sake of distinctness, to fix on some date which will nearly represent what we know, I should say 700 B.C. probably may nearly represent the age of the earliest Greek peristylar temple. This period is long enough to admit of all the developments that took place afterwards—too long, in fact, if we consider what an imaginative and inventive people the Greeks always were. With them artistic development must have progressed with a rapidity unknown with the more sluggish nations of the North; and till we can measure this, our speculations on the subject must be the merest guess-work.

In like manner it is impossible to say whether the peristyle was an original invention of some native architect, or whether it was borrowed from abroad. If it were merely the plan that was involved in the change, it does not seem beyond the scope of some indigenous architect; but when we consider all the changes that it involved, it is hardly probable that any one would have ventured upon it; hardly, at least, without having seen something like it carried out successfully elsewhere. My own impression is that the original hint came, like that of the pillar, from Egypt. There are in that country a tolerably numerous class of quasi-peripteral temples, called *Mammeisi*; but it is doubtful if any, at least of existing examples, are of an early age, and even then, though their plans offer a tempting similarity, their other arrangements are essentially different. If any of the temples of Northern Egypt were still in existence, we might hope to be able to settle this question, as they were those with which the Greeks were naturally most familiar. It also happens, from their being built with brick or rubble piers, they were most likely to offer similarities with those in Greece. At present, however, I fear we must content ourselves with remarking, that the Greek visitors to Egypt may have been struck with the beautiful effect of the

---

[1] Metaponte, Duc de Luynes et F. J. Debacq. Paris, 1833, fol.

long colonnades which the Egyptians everywhere introduced, and may have desired to introduce a corresponding effect in the adornment of their own similar edifices, and it is to this cause that we owe the introduction of the colonnades that subsequently formed the principal ornament of all Greek temples.

The first and most important change involved by the introduction of a peristyle was the transference of the apparent parts of the roof arrangements of the temple from the top of the cella walls to a new position on the summit of a range of columns. Instead of being the end of a triple combination of timbers, the triglyph became a substantial stone ornament. The metope, being no longer wanted for lighting, became a square frame, to contain, in the best age, a plain stone slab or a sculptured group; but if we may trust Roman traditions, when first employed it contained vases, wreaths, ox's skulls, anything, in fact, that was considered ornamental, and would serve to adorn a space that was originally open, and which they seemed unwilling to fill up solidly, so as to obliterate all reminiscences of its former use.

The next was the imitation in stone of all the apparent parts which had hitherto been in wood, but which would have been manifestly inappropriate in their new position. In doing this it is curious to observe how honestly the Greek architects acknowledged the whole of this to be a mere surface decoration, devoid of all real meaning, by their mode of treating the reverse side of this screen of triglyphs and metopes. None of the features of the external decoration go through to the inside. The back of the entablature is quite unbroken, and shows none of the divisions of the front. If it had been a real copy of wooden forms, in their proper situation, it is almost impossible but that the framework which composed the triglyph should have been carried back to the cella wall. Instead of this, the back of the entablature is quite smooth, without any mark of the division into triglyphs and metopes being carried through to the back, which, in a real imitation in stone of woodwork, was inevitable. Instead, also, of these forms being repeated on the cella walls, which was also inevitable if two lines of constructive decoration had previously existed, we have a continuous frieze, as in the Parthenon, which does not even suggest a reminiscence of the external form which the entablature afterwards took. It is evident from this, that originally there was only one line of decoration existing on the top of a wall. When it was thought expedient to transfer the triglyphs and metopes to a range of columns, entirely separated from the actual roof, it only remained to carry up the original wall to the required height; and if thought necessary to treat it ornamentally, it could only be done, in good taste, by using only a plain wall-decoration. Of course when this transfer was made it was desirable that the colonnade should be as like a wall as possible. At least the designers thought so, and, like most inventors, employed means ten times greater than was afterwards found needful in order to secure the requisite strength for the new invention. This is well exemplified in the peristyle of the Temple of Artemis at Ortygia, which for that and other reasons I believe to be the oldest example of the completed Doric order we possess.[1] The pillars are only their own diameters apart, and the capital spread so much that the abaci almost touch one another, and the architrave is of exaggerated depth. The echinus too is of that full rounded form characteristic of a very early age. A section of it, in fact, would represent fairly a bracket capital, which, I fancy, was the early wooden expedient, and may, after all, be the secret which accounts for the invention of the echinus, if we are not allowed to ascribe it to the Egyptians.

My impression is that this example may be considered as old as 700 B.C., or nearly so, and therefore, if this is so, is the earliest example of the completed Greek Doric we are acquainted with. Ortygia was occupied by Corinthian and Dorian colonists as early as 738, and there seems no reason why they should not have commenced this temple shortly afterwards.[2]

34.—Temple of Artemis, Ortygia.
(From Serra di Falco.)

A second consequence of this transference of the simulated roofing arrangement, from the top of the wall to the pillars of the peristyle, was nearly as important, and more interesting from its bearing on the present subject. It is evident that so soon as it was effected the metopes in the original arrangement were obscured, even if not obliterated—were at all events no longer available for lighting the interior of the temple. An obvious way of meeting the difficulty, to a modern architect at least, would have been to open windows in the wall lower down. But this was not the way the Greeks set to work.[3] For some reason or other they always objected to any interference with the walls of the cellas. There are remains enough to show that these were generally, if not always, coloured; and my own impression is, that they were used as great frames on which were depicted scenes from the life or legends of the

---

[1] Serra di Falco, Antichità di Sicilia, vol. vi. pl. ix. fig. 3.
[2] Clinton, Fasti Hellenici, vol. i. p. 265.
[3] There is no material evidence of windows so placed in a Doric temple except in that at Agrigentum. But that temple is not peristylar, and so abnormal in its design that no argument can be drawn from its arrangement. In Ionic temples they are not unfrequent.

god to which the temple was dedicated, or devoted to painted processions or religious ceremonials, such as that sculptured on the frieze of the Parthenon. From being exposed to the weather in their present ruined state all these paintings have perished. There can, however, be little doubt that they once existed, and this rendered the utilization of the walls for lighting purposes inadmissible, even if it were not that the ingenuity of the Greek architects hit on a far better and more artistic method of meeting the difficulty. This was effected by raising, instead of lowering them, and by inserting improved internal metopes in the roof of these temples in the manner which will be easily understood from the annexed section of the temple at Ægina.

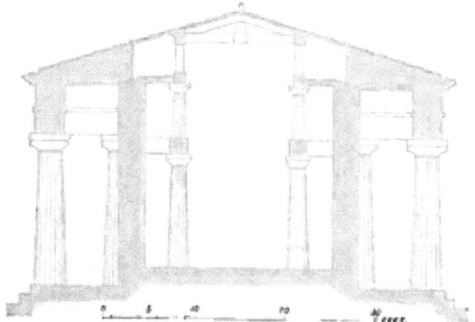

—Section of Temple at Ægina. (Twice the scale of Plan.)

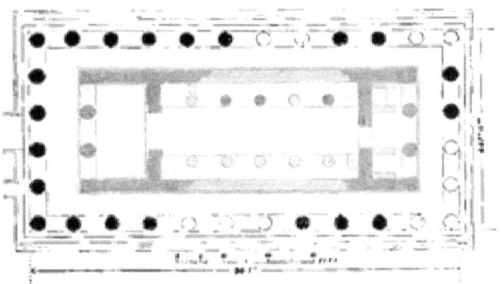

—Plan of Temple at Ægina. (From Cockerell.)

Any one who looks attentively at the plan of the temple at Ægina must be struck with the apparent absurdity of its arrangements as it at first sight appears. It consists of a small cella 24 feet by 42 feet—scarcely the size of ordinary London drawing-rooms—but designed to accommodate a statue of the god[1] which we know to have been colossal from the dimension of one of its eyes which was found on the spot. Notwithstanding this the floor is encumbered with two ranges of Doric columns two stories in height, reducing the available width to 13 feet. It was not to assist in carrying the roof that they were introduced, for at that time roofs 20 or 30 feet span, or even more, could have been no difficulty to Greek architects. Nor was it to support a gallery, because none existed—there was no room for one, the distance of the pillars from the wall being under 3 feet; but unless for the purpose of supporting a gallery, two ranges of columns standing on the heads of the other was a piece of bad and clumsy architecture that must have been nearly intolerable to Grecian taste. Of course, any expedient becomes tolerable, and even beautiful, when the reason is perfectly obvious. In this instance the motive was obvious enough, but the mode in which it was sought to accomplish it was clumsy, and at variance with all the principles of Greek architecture. If there had been a gallery it might have been forgiven, but without that excuse it was unpardonable. This was so much felt to be the case that it was remedied at Tegea and Bassae by the introduction of single Ionic and Corinthian columns extending to the roof; but in the early stages of the invention when only Doric columns were known or employed, there seemed no other mode of getting over the difficulty. In the meanwhile it seems evident that it could only have been adopted here to enable the architect to employ a very much slenderer columnar arrangement to support an internal metope or *opaion* instead of the stout column, which was indispensable for the external metope as shown in the last diagram. By this means they also obtained a higher light[2] than was before possible, and one that did not from any part of the temple strike directly on the spectator's vision, but must have illumined the whole with the most magical effect.

Before going further it may be as well to explain that the term the Greeks used to describe these internal metopes was Τὸ Ὀπαῖον. It is true the word is not so translated in our lexicons, but it is not to be expected that they would use

---

[1] I believe of the *goddess*, for though it generally bears the name of that of Jupiter Panhellenius, which was the name adopted by Cockerell in his beautiful work, the sculpture of the two pediments so evidently treats Minerva as the principal divinity in the action, that there seems no doubt that she was the deity to whom the temple was dedicated.

[2] In the woodcut I have adopted M. Garnier's dimensions as to height instead of Mr. Cockerell's. I have done so because Cockerell's attention does not seem to have been especially drawn to the subject, and he thought it of little importance, and quite sufficient, if from the few fragments of the upper range that remained, he could eke out an arrangement which would reach the roof, being fully impressed with the idea that the internal pillars were only a roofing expedient and nothing more. Garnier, on the contrary, examined the question with great care, and being quite impartial, was more likely to be right. He did not admit that there was any roof at all over the cella, and, using the experience gained at Paestum, was enabled to construct a combination much more in accordance with the principles of Greek architecture. (Revue Archéologique, tom. xi. p. 434.)

terms that would convey the true significance of what was not hitherto understood. But, before the present treatise is complete, it is hoped that the true meaning of the term will be apparent from what follows. "Opaion" will therefore be used throughout to describe an internal metope or clerestory opening, as contradistinguished from an hypæthron or skylight—the opaion being in all instances a vertical or perpendicular light, or window, the hypæthron always being used to describe a horizontal one cut out of the roof, which, so far as I know, was never in any instance used by any Greek architect, and, as before stated, only once by a Roman one, and that in a building which was not intended for a temple.

It may be a question whether all the six internal metopes were open at Ægina along the whole length of the cella (11 feet) with only a triglyph between them; or whether two were thrown together, making three openings on each side, or whether, in fact, the central two only were thrown together to light the statue, and the two end ones to light the temple. This could only be determined by making a model on sufficient scale to try the effect experimentally, but it is of little consequence at the present stage of the enquiry. We shall be able to form a better opinion after discussing the mode in which the Parthenon was lighted. My impression is that the central two only were open, forming one metope or opaion about 15 feet long by 4½ feet high, which in that climate would be ample for the purpose.

Unfortunately there is nothing among the remains found on the spot which aid in any way in determining this question. It is true Mr. Cockerell found a roofing tile—an imbrex—so formed that he concluded from its shape that it marked the end of an opening in the roof.¹ In this he was no doubt correct, but there is nothing to show that it could be applied only to a hole in the centre of the roof, as he supposed. It may as well have belonged to one of two or more openings on either side of the centre, as suggested in the accompanying woodcuts (Nos. 35, 36).

It may be anticipating a little on the regular chronological order of our argument, but it certainly will add to the clearness of what follows if, before going further, we describe the Temple of Apollo Epicurius at Bassæ, which is not only the most beautiful of all the temples known to us in Greece, excepting the Parthenon of course, but it is the temple of whose internal arrangements more has been ascertained than of any other. Fortunately too the plan of this temple and disposition of its interior, are in themselves quite sufficient to settle the question under discussion. If they do not prove that this temple was lighted by internal metopes there is little more to be said on the subject, but my impression is that when properly examined they establish the case beyond further cavil.²

---

¹ Cockerell's Ægina and Bassæ, plate vi. figs. 1 to 6.

² So I thought in 1849 when I published my "True Principles of Beauty in Art." In that work I engraved a plate No. IV. to illustrate the plan of this temple which I believed, and believe, to be the inevitable result of the form of the roof and mode of lighting. Had any one examined attentively that plate and read the accompanying text, in a fair spirit, the mode of lighting

In the first place, it seems impossible to study the plan of this temple, as shown in the woodcut, if with any care, without attention being drawn to certain peculiarities for which an explanation has never been even attempted, except by myself in the 'True Principles of Beauty in Art.' It is quite evident that it was not any constructive difficulty in the roof that compelled the contraction of the width of the cella from 22 feet to 14 feet, inasmuch as the same architect, Ictinus, was at the same time throwing a roof of 33 feet span over the central aisle of the Parthenon. It must therefore have been done for the same reason that the cella at Ægina was reduced from 21 feet to 13 feet. It is also evident that it was to avoid the architectural solecism of placing one pillar on the top of another— where there was no gallery—that the architect adopted here a taller Ionic order, and eked out the height by a complete entablature and tall frieze. This was one of the greatest strides in internal design made during the great age, and an

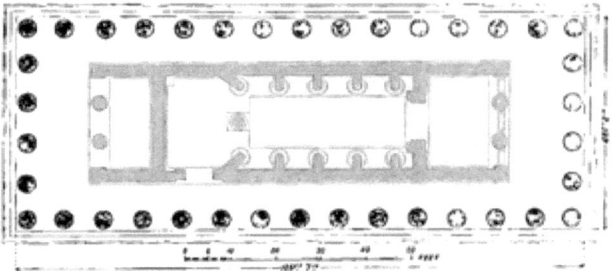

57.—TEMPLE OF APOLLO EPICURIUS AT BASSÆ. (From Cockerell.)

immense improvement on what preceded. But the most instructive feature of the plan is the spacing of the piers. Nothing can be more inartistic than the mode in which the inner piers—the southern ones—are thrust into the cella diagonally— the temple stands north and south instead of the usual arrangement of east and west —and nothing so clumsy as the mode in which the outer ones are jammed up against

Greek temples would have been settled there and then. So far as I know no one has done so in this country, at least nothing has appeared in print. On the continent it was hardly to be expected. Messrs. Hittorff and Chipiez probably never saw the book and cannot consequently be blamed for neglecting it. Frenchmen do not read foreign books, and though the Germans are supposed to read everything, their contempt for English archæology is such that they would hardly condescend to notice it. In this country the absolute indifference with which such controversies are regarded is an insuperable barrier to gaining a hearing on such a subject, and I have no hopes of plate No. II. of this work, which is an improved edition of the plate No. IV. in the former one, meeting with more attention than its predecessor. Greater knowledge of Greek architecture has enabled me to make considerable improvement in the details, though there is no alteration in the principles on which the former plate was constructed.

the northern wall next the entrance, unless compelled by some imperative necessity. It is evident that if regarding the internal arrangements only, any architect would have spaced the pillars equally along each side of the cella. The fact is the position of the internal pillars could be perceived from the exterior, and it was indispensable that each should be spaced exactly between two of the external columns irrespective of the internal arrangements. This, it is evident, could only be the case if there were windows in the roof, whose position could be seen from the outside, in conjunction with the peristyle. On any other theory that has been or seems to me capable of being suggested, the arrangement of these internal pillars is anomalous and clumsy to an extent of which we cannot conceive Ictinus being guilty.

The Parthenon at Athens was placed so high that its roof could not be seen — as will presently be explained — from any locality, not only in the Acropolis, but

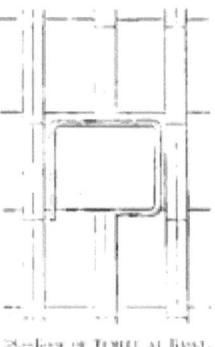

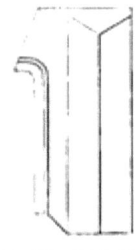

even in the city, and could only be perceived from hills so distant that its peculiarities could hardly be detected. The external arrangement of its roof, and the spacing of its opaion could in consequence easily be made subservient to those of the interior. But in a temple like this one at Bassæ, situated in a valley, and where the roof was looked down upon on all sides, its design was as important as that of the peristyle, and any want of harmony between the two must instantly have been detected, and been intolerable in so perfect a design. It was evidently to avoid this defect that the arrangements of the interior were sacrificed to the symmetry of the exterior, and the openings in the roof made to correspond with the intercolumniation of the peristyle.

From the disposition of the pillars and of the roofing-tiles, it seems clear that there were not more than four openings, in each side of the ridge of the roof. It may, however, be a question whether they were of the form shown in Plate II., or as drawn in the annexed woodcut (No. 38). A tile was found by Mr. Cockerell, and figured by him on Plate VII., Fig. 2, and reproduced in the annexed woodcut, which shows the angle of one of these openings. Another is said to have been found by Baron Haller, which doubtfully indicates both the upper and lower corners as being curved, but neither contradicts the theory that two tiles were

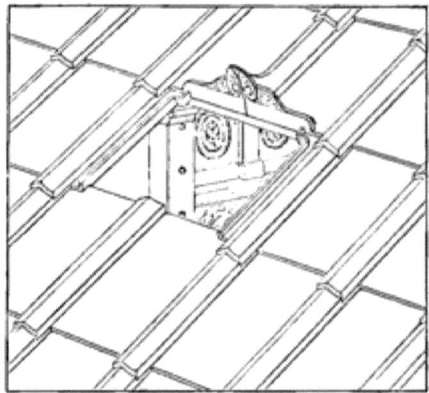

40.—ISOMETRIC VIEW OF OPENING IN ROOF, ÆGINA.

not comprehended in one opening[1] instead of one. Whether there was an acroterium in front of the imbrex as shown in the annexed woodcut, or whether it was cut off abruptly, is a question not easy to decide. The last woodcut (No. 38)

---

[1] Sessional Papers, Royal Institute of Brit. Arch., 1864–5, p. 53. It is not quite clear how far the Baron's sketch is to be depended upon. It seems only to have been an eye sketch, either in pencil or with a pen, and never worked out or drawn to scale. The upper curve is quite certain; it is identical with that drawn by Mr. Cockerell, but the lower cusp is, to say the least of it, doubtful. It does not, however, in the least degree interfere with the theory just explained, and may easily be adapted to the opinion (woodcut No. 38), as shown on the right-hand side of the opening. Only one does not see its use, and the Greeks never did anything without a motive.

In this paper the late John Wyatt Papworth describes the roof of this temple in a manner which is a curious illustration of how difficult it is for British architects to consider their Grecian brethren as other than incompetent bunglers. He first explains, as Cockerell had done before him, how the Greeks had chiselled away half the thickness of the tiles, and with infinite pains and at a great expense attached the imbrex to the tile in one piece, so as to form a perfectly watertight joint between the two tiles. This was done here more perfectly than in any other temple of Greece. But having accomplished this Mr. Papworth represents Ictinus as cutting a hole in the field of his tiles, occupying about two-thirds of its whole area, through which the rain might pour into the cella of the temple, at its own sweet will, without let or hindrance! It was not thus I conceive that the greatest of Greek architects went to work.

represents the opening as if the Greeks attempted to hide it, which I conceive quite contrary to the spirit of their architecture. They must, I conceive, have marked it externally, but whether in the manner shown in the plate and in woodcut 40, or in any other, I am not prepared to say, and this need not here be discussed, as it is of no importance to the main question.

Although from the disposition of the pillars internally, and the form of the tiles, it is nearly certain that there were only four openings on each side externally, it may be considered as an open question whether the three intermediate spaces were also open internally. If there was any doubt as to the sufficiency of light introduced through the four represented as open in Plate II., there might be some hesitation, but I think any one looking at this isometric view may convince himself, as I have done, that this area was ample for the purpose. Indeed, I fancy that a very much closer grille than I have suggested must have been introduced to subdue the excess, and complete, in appearance, the decoration of the interior.

There are, besides, reasons which render it nearly certain that the intermediate metopes were closed. On looking attentively at the elevation of the capital as shown in Cockerell's Plate XIII., it will be observed that in front, but not at the sides, there are two brackets introduced which look like the commencement of a pilaster, or at least suggest such an addition on the top of the capital. Nothing of that sort could exist here, in consequence of the frieze intervening; but nothing in Greek architecture was inserted at hap-hazard, or suggested without a motive, and these brackets seem certainly to indicate that a pilaster was introduced somewhere above them—not in this instance in immediate connexion constructively, but artistically to suggest a connexion between the capital and something that was above it.[1]

The introduction of a pilaster in the intermediate spaces has the further advantage of suggesting a truss over each pillar, so dividing the roof into three compartments, which without this would run the risk of being slightly monotonous, but with a pilaster and truss over each pillar, the whole design of the roof, it appears to me, would be singularly congruous and beautiful.

Throughout all these restorations I have adopted Mr. Cockerell's dimensions literally and without question, in order not to introduce any additional element of controversy. I am convinced, however, that his internal pillars are a foot, or at least 8 inches, too high. Unfortunately no internal pillar was found standing, and a sufficient number of drums did not exist, or were not measured, to enable any one to ascertain the height, from the curve of the enstasis as Mr. Penrose did so successfully for the pillars at Priene.[2] Mr. Donaldson makes their height a little less than that of the external columns, but he admits that he has no authority

---

[1] I am indebted for the suggestion of this pilaster to my friend Mr. Stannus, who made the drawing for Plate II.
[2] Antiquities of Ionia, vol. iv. p. 56, et seqq.

for this. "The height," he says, "of the internal column is presumed,"¹ and Blouet renders it doubtful by applying two different scales to his two plates, representing the interior, and, as is too often the case in French works, does not quote any dimensions.² Mr. Cockerell makes the height of the external column 19 feet 5 inches, of the internal 20 feet 5 inches. My impression is that they were equal, or very nearly so, because in the first place it would be a more pleasing proportion for a pillar carrying a heavy frieze, and in the second place because I think Ictinus would certainly insist on the metopes being exactly square. But there may have been other ways of adjusting this that I have not thought of, but which some other restorer may suggest.

When Pausanias said the roof of "this temple is of stone,"³ he evidently did not mean only that its roof was covered with marble tiles like almost all the temples of Greece at that period. He must have referred to some peculiarity in the roof of this temple, which was worthy of remark. Nor is it difficult to see what this was, for on examining carefully the remains, it seems tolerably obvious that the marble covering of the roof was seen from the interior as well as from the exterior, and this could not have been generally the case with Greek temples. At least, if I am correct in supposing that the tiles were generally laid in a ceiling or lining of cedar, or at least of timber planking.

If the disposition of the tiles in this temple is carefully examined, it will be seen (Plate II.) that on each side of the ridge there is one full tile and two half tiles, disposed in the most careful manner, so as to form a perfectly symmetrical roof when looked at from the interior. This could hardly be the result of accident, but must have been a part of the original design. I have suggested that they were adorned with painting, because there is a tile in the British Museum brought from Achaia by Colonel Leake, which shows that it was painted on the under side,⁴ and must have belonged to a roof constructed as I suppose that one was.⁵ It is true this tile in the British Museum, though of the same shape as the marble tiles, is in terra-cotta, but in this instance it is fortunately so, as it retains its colouring in all its original freshness, which has been entirely washed off from those in marble.⁶

According to appearances the rafters which supported these tiles were of

---

¹ Antiquities of Athens, vol. v. p. 14 of his Memoir.
² Expédition Scientifique de la Morée, vol. ii. pls. 28 and 29.
³ Arcadia, viii. ch. 41, λίθου καὶ αὐτὸς ὄροφος.
⁴ It is figured in detail in Hittorff's Architecture Antique de la Sicile, pl. 83.
⁵ It is true Pliny tells us that Brietis was the first to paint lacunaria (ceilings?) in this manner. He lived long after this temple was built, but there is no doubt but the lacunaria of the Parthenon and at Ægina were adorned with coloured patterns originally, so that either Pliny was mistaken or his expression misunderstood.
⁶ In their recent excavations at Olympia the Germans have found numerous fragments of acroteria and cymatia, in terra-cotta, richly decorated in colour, but not one fragment of marble so treated. Yet it seems impossible that a monochromatic and polychromatic architecture should simultaneously have existed side by side in the same place. Bœtticher, Olympia, pl. v.

wood, and, if so, they must have been richly painted to accord with the higher tone of decoration of the rest of the temple, and if they were so coloured, it is most probable that the soffites were so also. It may, however, be suggested that they were of marble, and that the expression of Pausanias, ἐν λίθῳ, requires this. There would be no constructive difficulty involved in this suggestion. These rafters are only 8 feet in length, and there are roofing-stones found in the lacunaria both of the pronaos and posticum, which exceed 12 feet. It is extremely improbable, however, that the Greeks should have employed stone for so essentially a wooden form of construction, and, if they had, it is almost impossible that some fragment should not have been found on the floor of the temple among the ruins.

Whatever conclusion we may come to regarding these and other details, which do not concern us here, one thing is certain, that the more this temple is studied the more exquisite does it appear, and if it was inferior in beauty to that at Tegea, which Pausanias declares it was, we certainly have lost in that last-named temple something that would give us a higher idea of Greek architecture than we can gather from any remains now existing, though these are generally admitted to be more worthy of admiration than any known to exist elsewhere.

From the remote and secluded situation of this temple it is probable that the image of the god was a mere "simulacrum," which had become sacred from some accidental cause among the rude inhabitants of the mountain. It probably was placed in the inner part of the temple, where it was not dependent on any particular mode of lighting, but stood facing the east, and apparently received sufficient light through the doorway in front of it. Indeed, all the arrangements of the temple seem to indicate that the image of the god, though probably the most sacred, was not, artistically, the most prominent object in the temple, and was consequently made subordinate to the more important architectural features of the design.

The image of the god certainly was not placed in the cella, as is usual in Greek temples, which may account for some of the peculiarities in plan of this one. The only ornament of the cella here, so far as we can see, was an important frieze, which is now in the British Museum, and all that was required was that this should be perfectly lighted. This was accomplished by a cross light falling full upon it from the east and the west, so high that the direct rays of the sun never fell on the eyes of a spectator standing on the floor of the temple. If there was any danger of this it could be easily obviated by introducing a cymatium, as is suggested by Mr. Cockerell, but without a model it is difficult to determine that question. So far as I can judge, from diagrams, the mode of lighting suggested by Plate II. is nearly perfect. I know, however, of no temple (except the Parthenon) of which it would be more desirable to construct a model than of this one. It is evidently so nearly perfect a gem that a great deal would be sure to be learnt from a more complete study of it, than can be made from mere diagrams. It would be easy to construct it, for all the materials are available. But who is likely to undertake it?

Now that we are enabled to understand the arrangements of the Temple of Minerva Alea at Tegea, we gather that they must have been similar to those at Bassae, but the internal order there being Corinthian, this would lend itself more kindly to its position than the Ionic, which could not be used without very considerable modification. It is much to be regretted that scarcely anything remains of this temple, for though Pausanias was clearly mistaken in saying that it was the largest in the Peloponnesus,[1] he probably was justified in his estimate of it as the most beautiful. Nowhere, certainly, were the three orders so exquisitely combined—a Doric peristyle, and a Corinthian order in the interior, with the Ionic in the pronaos and posticum, as it was used in the Temple of Ceres at Paestum, in a combination similar to that employed in the propylæa at Athens and Eleusis.[2] The three orders were also employed simultaneously in the Parthenon, but, owing to the exigencies of the building, not so happily combined as at Tegea. If Ictinus could produce so beautiful an interior as he did at Bassae, by the use of the somewhat intractable Ionic order, it is easy to conceive how vast an improvement the employment of the Corinthian would have been, and how exquisite the result. The destruction of the specimens of the Corinthian order, as used then, is a loss to art that nothing now can probably replace. It may have been less rich than the Roman examples, but the elegance of the few specimens we have in Athens and at Didyme makes us regret that we have no more. The recovery of those at Tegea would no doubt have justified the encomium of Pausanias, but it is to be feared it is hopeless to expect to find them, the temple being so utterly destroyed.

As the so-called Temple of Neptune at Paestum retains more of the internal arrangement *in situ* than any other Doric temple that is known to us, its remains would suffice to settle many disputed points, if we only had any drawings of it on which we could depend. Unfortunately the locality is unhealthy, and artists seem never to have lingered long enough there to finish their drawings on the spot, and verify them from the existing remains. Those of La Gardette, published at the end of the last century,[3] were made before minute accuracy was

[1] Pausanias, book viii. 45.

[2] Up to a very recent date all the world were agreed that from Pausanias's description this must have been an Ionic temple. Herr Milchhöfer (Mittheilungen des Arch. Inst. zu Athen, 1er Heft, 1880) was, I believe, the first to suggest the truth, by restricting the word ναός to its literal but perfectly legitimate signification. By this happy suggestion the whole was reduced to order in perfect accord with all the principles of Greek art, which the previous translation offended to a painful extent. Having fully explained in a note on page 2 of the Introduction to the 4th volume of the Antiquities of Ionia, published last year, how the correction should be made, it need not be repeated here, as no material remains exist to throw light on the subject we are now investigating.

[3] La Gardette, Ruines de Paestum, Paris, 1799.

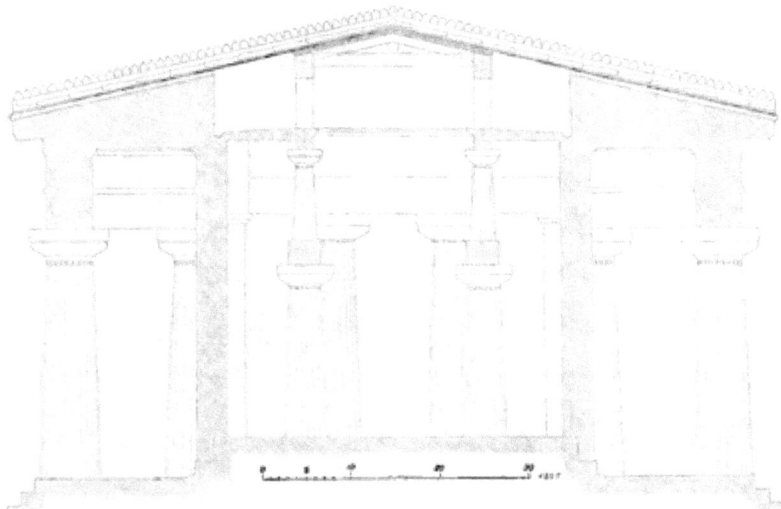

41.—Section of the Temple of Neptune at Pæstum. (Double the scale of Plan.)

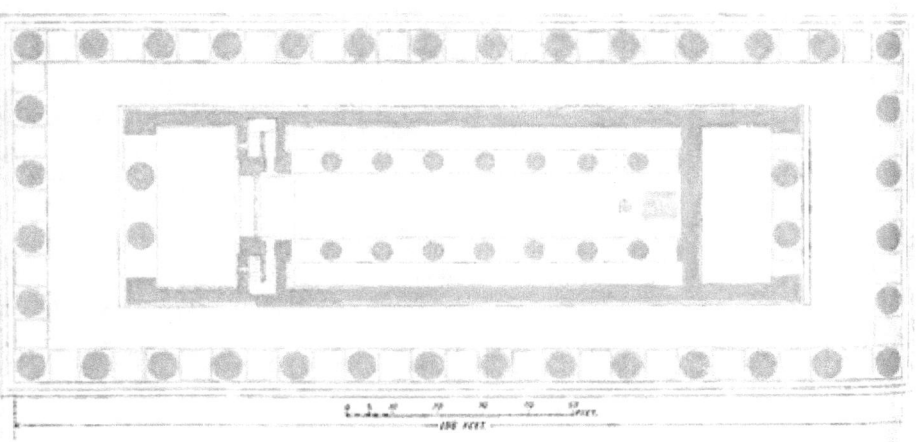

42.—Plan of Temple of Neptune at Pæstum. (From Labrouste.) (Same scale as the other Greek temples.)

thought indispensable; and those of Labrouste, published five years ago by the École des Beaux Arts with all the luxury and splendour of engraving which characterizes works published under the auspices of the French Government,[1] are by no means to be depended upon. The different plates contradict one another, and none of them stand the photographic test. Those published by Wilkins[2] seem to have been made with great care, but the plates are without scales, and very important measurements are frequently misquoted in the figured dimensions, so that it is impossible ever to be sure that you are quoting him correctly. Those, however, given below are figured in both works. Notwithstanding these difficulties, I believe the annexed section very nearly represents the actual facts of the case.

Fortunately there is no doubt about the plan of the temple, nor of the external order of the pillars. The great difficulty is to ascertain the height from the ground, and the form of the upper architrave internally. Labrouste makes the total height 11·10 metres, or 36 feet 6 inches; Wilkins, 19·9 + 11 + 3·6 = 34·3 feet, which is probably nearer the truth. Labrouste seems to have been possessed with the idea that they supported a roof which he makes solid throughout, without any opening whatever, and may have stretched the dimensions to reach what, according to his theory, was the true state of the case. Wilkins had no theory, and his Plate 10 shows that he must have measured this internal order with great care. But more important than even its height from the ground is the form of this upper architrave. All the drawings I have had access to, represent it as the same on both sides. The photographs, on the contrary, represent it thus (woodcut 43); and this is confirmed by two string courses on the end walls of the temple, twenty inches apart, as their presence can only be explained by the one corresponding to the inner, the other to the outer, face of the architraves. If this is so, the mode of roofing and lighting this temple is quite without difficulty. All the parts fit easily together, and the proportions are exactly what is wanted. If the architrave is not notched, as represented in the last woodcut, there would be a certain clumsiness in the construction, not indeed sufficient to affect the theory of the mode of lighting, which besides may be owing to its being an early and a provincial example. If, however, on examination, it should turn out that the architrave is of the form represented in the last woodcut, it is the most distinct material proof yet found of the theory I am advocating, and, as far as one example can go, final in its correctness. The result must be, that the light was introduced as shown in the annexed section, which meets all the exigencies of the case in so far as they can be at present ascertained. At Bassæ the evidence is probably equally conclusive, but

[1] Labrouste, Temples de Pæstum, Paris, 1877.   [2] Wilkins's Magna Græcia, London, 1807.

it is derived from reasoning from the plan. Unfortunately there are no material remains of the roof in that temple that bear on the subject either way.

One of the hitherto unexplained peculiarities of the temple is the height to which the floor of the cella is raised above that of the peristyle, which exceeds 6 feet. If, as Labrouste supposes, the only light was introduced by the doorway, this would diminish the amount by nearly one-half, and otherwise would have been a most objectionable feature. But if the intention was to raise the floor sufficiently for the internal screen of columns to reach the epaion without becoming excessive or clumsy in their dimensions, it is intelligible. I cannot suggest any other explanation of the peculiarity, and I am not aware of any theory which even pretends to explain why it was adopted.

The greatest interest, however, that attaches to the temple at Paestum arises from its being an almost exact counterpart of the celebrated Temple of Jupiter at Olympia; and without the aid of its more complete remains, we should hardly be able to understand even approximately how the Olympian temple was arranged. Nothing of the superstructure now remains, but the recent German excavations have disclosed the entire ground plan, and proved its identity with that of the Paestum temple in all essential respects, and where they differ the differences are almost more instructive than the similarities.

The result of the latest German investigations[1] tends to the belief that the temple at Elis was commenced about the year 469, and completed 457, and that the chryselephantine statue by Phidias was placed in it 438 B.C. My own impression is that nothing has yet been brought forward to invalidate the date assigned to it by Pausanias, who certainly seems to say that it was designed by Libon, a native architect, in the 52nd Olympiad, 570.[2] If, at the same time, we may assume, which a passage in Herodotus[3] seems to imply, that the Paestum temple was commenced after the 59th Olympiad, 543, we come so nearly to the date we should assign to these two temples from their style and peculiarities, that I cannot but fancy that the middle of the sixth century B.C. is more nearly correct. There are several peculiarities which seem to show that the design of the Paestum temple was adopted after the experience gained at Olympia. The internal pillars there are 6 feet in diameter, which is no doubt excessive, but at Paestum, as above pointed out, by raising the floor 6 feet the builders were enabled to reduce this dimension to 4 feet 6 inches and still reach the opaion; the external walls were also reduced from 4 feet to 3 feet 4 inches, thus so far adding to the spaciousness of the interior, and, with the smaller diameter of the columns, affording a decided improvement.

The dimensions of the temple at Elis are slightly in excess of those at Paestum, being 212 feet in length by 90 across, as compared with 196 by 80 feet, and the

---

[1] Ulrichs, Halle, 1867, quoted in Krell, Dorischenstyl, Stuttgart, 1870, p. 85.
[2] Pausanias, v. ch. 10, 3.   [3] Herodotus, i. 67.

great part of this difference in section is given to the central aisle, which at Elis is 21 feet 6 inches as against 15 feet only. Even with this extension, however, it is difficult to understand how Phidias managed to treat with dignity a colossal chryselephantine figure of the god, seated on a throne, adorned with all the adjuncts described by Pausanias. At Athens the figure of Minerva was erect and unencumbered, and a space 33 feet in width, which was there assigned to the statue, was probably as much as was required for its adequate display; but 21 feet for a larger seated figure is a difficulty which no one has yet been able to explain. Those attempts at restoration that have hitherto been made are by no means satisfactory. Perhaps the Germans, who were employed in the excavations, when they have leisure, will apply themselves to the solution of the problem. They have skill in drawing and learning to any extent, and with the knowledge they acquired during their explorations they certainly approach the task with advantages which none have hitherto possessed. If they succeed they will worthily close the cycle which was commenced by the publication of Quatremère de Quincy's 'Jupiter Olympien.' That work failed principally for want of local knowledge, which certainly cannot be pleaded in excuse at the present day.

One peculiarity of the Olympian temple, as described by Pausanias, is worthy of notice. He mentions internal staircases, in the aisles probably, which led to galleries (ὑπερῷον) "by which access was had to the statue,"[1] and from that, a winding stair (σκολία) led to the roof. As no trace of these stairs was found in the excavations, they were probably in wood, and must have been awkward in the extreme. At Pæstum the stone staircases, as in most Sicilian temples, were inserted in the thickness of the walls, on either side of the entrance, and led direct to the opaion. But whether this arose from the Pæstum temple having no galleries, or was adopted as an improvement on the Olympian example, is not quite clear. But whichever view we adopt it shows that easy and constant access to the roof by the attendants of the temple was an indispensable adjunct to a Grecian temple, and if it was not to adjust the blinds and screens of an opaion, it is difficult to say why it was provided.

It would require a model to be made on a considerable scale, in order to ascertain exactly what amount of light was required by either of these two temples, or at what point it should be admitted so as to light the statue most artistically. It is evident, however, that the means of doing so are in excess of what is required, and that the architect could in consequence play with the construction and admit the light wherever he thought best, and where it was most convenient for the drainage of the roof and other necessities. The refinement of adjusting the external openings to the spacing of the peristyle was not apparently thought of when these two temples were erected; it is a refinement that may not

---

[1] Pausanias, v. 10.

have been introduced when they were built, or it may have been that the temples were not so situated on the plains, that the roofs could be easily seen from any locality in their immediate neighbourhood. This certainly was the case at Paestum, and partially so, at least, at Elis.

We must wait till the results of the German excavations are published in greater detail before hazarding a decided opinion regarding this temple; but so far as can be judged from the data at present available, it was the clumsiest piece of architecture in all Greece. We have long known that its sculptures are very inferior to any others we know of the great age to which they belong, and must have been the work of local sculptors, only under the direction of Alcamenes and Paionius. Architecture, however, does not generally vary so much from individual idiosyncrasies, and it is most strange, unless in a very early age, that it should be so inferior to what we might expect. In the meantime, however, as so little of the Olympian temple remains above the foundation, it is an immense gain to archaeology that we have a sister temple at Paestum, which is so nearly perfect as it is. By comparing the two we are enabled to supply to the one what is wanted in the other, and so make an immense stride in our knowledge of the architecture of Greek temples.

The Heraion at Olympia, though smaller, is architecturally even a more interesting temple than the great temple itself. What we know of it is entirely owing to the German excavations, as even its site was before unknown, and when the whole details of these discoveries are made known the results may be even more valuable than they now appear to be.

The temple was hexastyle, but with the very unusual number of 16 columns on the flanks, as shown in the annexed plan, making its dimensions 145 feet in length against 57 in width,¹ which is, I believe, the largest relative proportion of any temple in Greece proper. The design of some of the pillars of the peristyle is very old—as old nearly as those of the Temple of Artemis at Syracuse (woodcut 34). Others are as modern, or more so, than those of the great temple² itself, showing an extent of alterations since the original design which is perplexing. The interior, however, seems to have been entirely remodelled at a very recent period, and is one of the most regular of any found in Greece, though so very little of it remains that it is not easy to feel sure about all its details. The most marked peculiarity, as will be seen from the plan, is that the pillars of the interior are spaced with the same interval of 11 feet with those of the exterior, and correspond with these in position, one internal pillar being placed in the axis of each of those of the peristyle. At Bassae one pillar of

---

¹ There is a discrepancy of nearly 10 feet between the figured dimensions and the scale on the plate, which renders the exact determination of these dimensions doubtful.
² Ausgrabungen zu Olympia, pl. xxxiv., ix. and x.

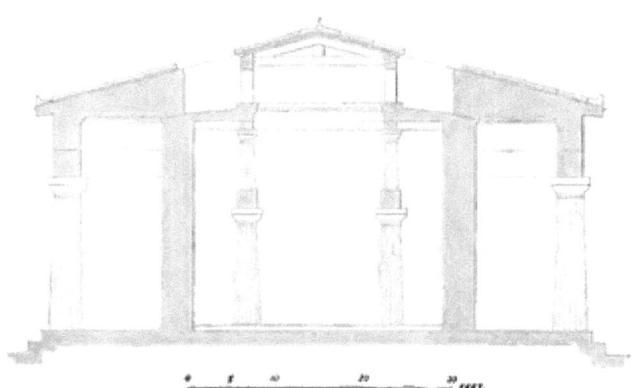

44.—Restored Section of the Heraion, Olympia.

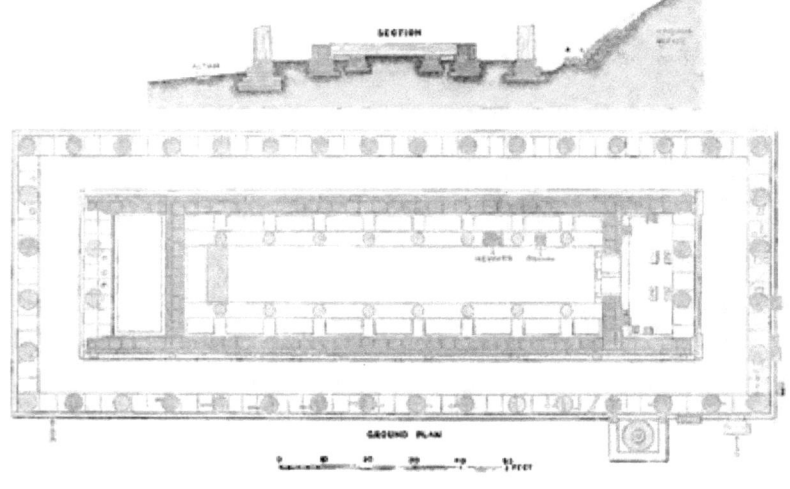

45.—Plan and Section of the Heraion, Olympia. (From the German Excavations.)

the interior was placed between two of the exterior in a manner that strikes the eye from the awkwardness it produces in the plan, owing to the restricted area of the cella. Here from the length of the cella it was easily adjusted; but the motive was evidently the same. The Mount Kronos was immediately adjacent to the temple and overlooked the roof, so that any discrepancy between the external and internal columns, as evidenced by the openings in the roof, would be simply intolerable to a Greek eye, and must therefore be avoided. The difference between placing the internal columns opposite, instead of between the external columns, enabled the architect to employ larger metopes, and to treat the whole more freely and artistically, which in this case was indispensable. As we learn from Pausanias, the Heraion was much more of a statue gallery, than a temple for the display of one image of a god or goddess, and nothing can have been better arranged for its purpose than this temple was. At Bassæ there was only a frieze, and the light, if sufficient, might be introduced anywhere; here its quantity and the angle at which it fell were all-important. It was fortunate that the Germans found the statue of Hermes, by Praxiteles, and the statue of the Roman lady in the position which they originally occupied, which is exactly that which from the disposition of the architecture we might be led to expect.[1]

This temple is interesting to us from an anecdote told by Pausanias,[2] which in itself would, I conceive, be sufficient to prove my case if it were open to argument. When Elis was attacked by the Lacedæmonians, some soldiers undertook to defend this temple against an attack from Mount Kronos, which was adjacent to it (see section), and from a military point of view completely commanded it. For this purpose they manned the opaion, which, as will be seen by the section on the previous page, was admirably adapted for the purpose. If indeed the temple had been built as a fortification it could not be better adapted for the purposes of defence than it was. While the fight was going on a hoplite who was wounded crept for protection into the space between the keramaria and the tiles, and having been left there when his companions were either beaten or retired, his body—dried to a mummy—was long afterwards found and buried outside the city. On any theory of a skylight or horizontal opening in the roof, the story is simply inexplicable and absurd. Assuming the

---

[1] We are now proposing to erect a Museum of Casts. For this purpose we cannot do better than copy the interior of this temple. We may depend upon it the Greeks knew better than we do how their sculptures ought to be lighted, and we cannot do wrong in copying them as literally as possible. They are now erecting galleries for casts at Cambridge, and I am not without hopes that one of them will be a copy of the interior of the Heraion, and that we may thus have an opportunity of judging of the effect of the Hermes, placed and lighted as it was done by Praxiteles himself.

[2] Pausanias, v. 20. 2.

section to be as shown in the last woodcut (44) the whole follows naturally as a matter of course, and in so far proves that it is correct.

Another circumstance is mentioned in the same chapter by Pausanias, which bears directly on the subject we are now treating of. In the opisthodomos was preserved one of the wooden columns of the original house, Œnomaus, which was alone preserved when it was burned by lightning. From the narrative it is not quite clear whether it was *in situ* as one of the pillars of the existing temple, or whether it was merely preserved there as a curiosity. The latter now seems the most probable, as the Germans found the temple complete with all its columns of stone, and there was in consequence no place where a wooden one could be used. But even if this is so, it is interesting as confirming the views above expressed (p. 56) of wooden columns being used in the original temples of Greece, both in the pronaos and posticum, before the introduction of the peristylar arrangement.

It would be tedious as well as unprofitable to attempt to explain how light was introduced into all the smaller hexastyles in Sicily and elsewhere. Once it is admitted that all Greek temples were lighted by internal metopes in the roof, we may safely trust to the ingenuity of the Greek architects for having effected this in the most advantageous and artistic manner. If the theory is not admitted, after the above explanation, "cadit quæstio," nothing that could now be adduced would avail anything, though I see no difficulty in the matter anywhere. But in some temples where a range of internal columns probably once existed, as in the temple of Theseus at Athens, they have been removed when the temple was converted into a church. When this conversion was effected the three upper courses of the walls, internally, were cut away so as to allow of a vault being thrown across the nave, in place of the wooden roof that originally existed there. In doing this these early Christians obliterated all traces of the mode in which the original roof was constructed, so that what is one of the most complete of all the temples now existing in Greece is of no avail for elucidating the question that now occupies us. Even the floor has been replaced by one of concrete of modern construction, so that we cannot even trace whether there were then any pillars existing, much less what their position may have been.[1]

Singularly enough, while the internal arrangements of the Theseion, which is the most complete of Greek temples, have been so completely obliterated that it is of no use whatever for our present purposes, the temple at Assos, which it is not an exaggeration to say, is the least perfect of any, affords us a hint which may be of value in this investigation. Mr. Clarke and a party of American archæologists have recently excavated and delineated this temple with

---

[1] I owe these facts to a section of the temple made for me by Herr Dörpfeld, at Dr Schliemann's instance.

the most praiseworthy diligence [1] and exactness. Literally not one stone of the temple remains *in situ* above the foundations; but on the floor of the cella they found a mosaic pavement, the dimensions of which are perfectly defined. The ornamental part of it is 13 feet wide, and the space between the outer face of the cella walls and the pavement is between 6 feet 6 inches and 6 feet 9 inches, or as nearly as may be the distance between the outside of the walls and the inner lines of the cella at Bassæ.

From this I gather that there were internal pillars or pilasters, which thickened the external walls of the cella to the extent of 7 feet at least, which could only have been done if it were wanted to support an opaion or some contrivance for lighting the cella.

One of the most interesting points about this temple is, that it is adorned with sculptures of so archaic a character,[2] that if found in Sicily or Greece we should be inclined to carry back its date to 600 B.C. or thereabouts; but there is reason for believing that it is not much older than the Theseion, which in plan and in architectural details it so much resembles. Mr. Clarke is of opinion that it cannot be dated before the Battle of Mycale,[3] 475 B.C., and he seems to be justified in the conclusion. If this is so, the dates of the history of sculpture in Greece must be revised to a considerable extent before any reliance can be placed upon them.

To return, however, from this digression, it is evident that in many temples the pillars were probably wooden posts and have consequently perished, and in others, where the cellas were very narrow, the light may have been introduced in the upper part of the cella walls, as in the original wooden temples, and the drainage managed above the pteroma walls, which could easily be done. But in all these instances the mode of effecting it, if explained by a modern architect, though it might afford a striking proof of his ingenuity and taste, would prove nothing. In all those cases where the temple is so completely ruined that no trace of the original form of the roof remains, it is idle to speculate on how it may have been formed, except from analogy with more fortunate examples. By confining our researches to those temples only which possess some material remains to guide us, we are much less liable to be led astray, and even if wrong, the materials exist in such cases of testing the truth of our speculations, and correcting such errors as we may be led into. In a general work on Grecian Doric architecture it might be necessary to describe many temples of which all mention is here omitted; but, in a special work on their mode of illumination, it seems more expedient to confine what we have to say to those temples whose remains tend to elucidate the subject we are investigating.

---

[1] Investigations at Assos, by J. T. Clarke, Boston, 1882.

[2] All the sculptures that were found at Assos are now in the Louvre, having been sent there by M. Texier.

[3] Clarke in loc.

CHAPTER V.

ABNORMAL GREEK TEMPLES.

In the preceding Chapter an attempt was made to explain the change that became necessary in the form of Greek temples by the introduction of the peristylar arrangement, and the consequent modification in the mode of lighting. In so far as is necessary to describe the Greek hexastyle temples, as an introduction to the Parthenon, the above might suffice, but there are in Greece and Sicily several temples of abnormal design, but at the same time so interesting from their dimensions and design, that it is impossible to pass them over, in a work like the present, without at least some attempt to elucidate their peculiarities.

The first of these is the great Temple of Jupiter at Agrigentum, which has the bad pre-eminence of being, although one of the largest, at the same time the least artistic temple the Greeks ever erected. It is 357 feet in length by 170 feet, but is wholly astylar. Instead of a peristyle, it is enclosed by a screen of half-columns joined by a wall between. Being principally erected with small stones which could easily be removed, this temple has been more than usually subject to the depredations of the neighbouring villagers, so that now very little remains above ground, and that little has been so carelessly explored and described that it is very difficult to make out some features of the design. There is great uncertainty, for instance, as to the situation and form of the entrance. Serra di Falco removes the central half-column on the east front, and replaces it by a great doorway 24 feet wide by 48 feet in height,[1] which is a nearly impossible feature in so microlithic

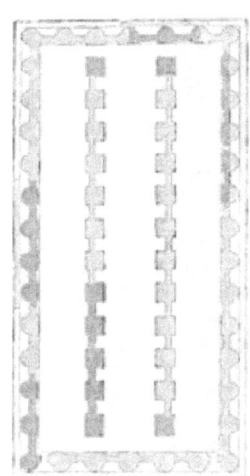

46.—PLAN OF THE GREAT TEMPLE AT AGRIGENTUM. (From Cockerell. Scale 100 feet to 1 inch.)

a temple, and a most disagreeable one. Cockerell, on the contrary, introduces two small doorways (see woodcut) 9 feet by 20 feet in height between the

---

[1] Antichità di Sicilia, vol. iii. pl. xxvi.

outer inter-columniation,[1] which is, to say the least of it, the most undignified way ever proposed for entering a Greek temple. My own impression is that there were six doorways in the principal or eastern front; one probably round each corner, and several—without examination of the ruins it is impossible to say how many—on each flank, and Mr. Cockerell's two were probably introduced at the west. Not being a peristylar temple the architect must most probably have sought to give it practically as much of the convenience and effect of a peristylar arrangement as possible. But for convenience of access and beauty of design he must, I conceive, have multiplied his openings to the utmost possible extent the construction of the temple admitted of. Six doorways 10 feet wide by 20 feet high would have formed a dignified entrance to even this temple, especially when preceded by a handsome flight of steps, which we know was the case, extending across the front.

The interior of the temple was divided into three parts by longitudinal walls, and consisted of two aisles each 37 feet wide, which seem to have been used by the Sicilians as a promenade—a sort of exchange in fact—only remotely connected with the temple.[2] The temple, properly so called, consisted of a hieron or cella, 58 feet across internally (Diodorus calls it 60 feet[3]), and 68 feet 8 inches including the outer walls. The internal space was again contracted by buttresses to 45 feet, in order to render it more easy to put a roof upon it. This, however, was never completely carried out, according to Diodorus, in consequence of the wars which supervened before it was accomplished. It is admitted by all restorers that the aisles were lighted by a range of 38 windows between the ordinary half pillars just under the entablature. This, indeed, is what we would naturally expect in a temple where, as was the case in this instance, the object was not to light an image, and where there was no cella wall so protected from the atmosphere that could be decorated by paintings. Under such circumstances their presence where they are found was unobjectionable, and was exactly the expedient we at the present day would adopt for lighting such halls.

In the central part the light was certainly introduced between the telamones, which were placed high and immediately under the roof. There may be some difference of opinion as to the exact mode in which this was done. Generally the telamones are represented as single figures, one over each pillar, but that does not seem an artistic arrangement, and as the roof was necessarily an open timber one, it would necessitate the main trusses being 27 feet apart longitudinally,

---

[1] Antiquities of Athens, &c., 1830, vol. v. pl. i.
[2] Polybius, ix. ch. xxvii.
[3] Diodorus, xiii. 82. Winckelmann's suggestion to add the word ἐκτὸς to the text of Diodorus is one of those proposals to alter the text of an author, which are too common among antiquaries when they get into a difficulty they cannot explain, which are generally most mischievous and misleading. In this instance the plan of the temple enables us to choose any dimensions between 58 and 68 ft. to reconcile the text with the plan, according as we assume Diodorus meant external or internal dimensions of the nave.

CHAP. V.   ABNORMAL GREEK TEMPLES.   93

which is nearly impossible. If the telamones were placed in pairs, one on each side of the opening, as shown in the woodcut 48, it would allow of four trusses instead of two, and have altogether, it seems to me, a better effect when seen from

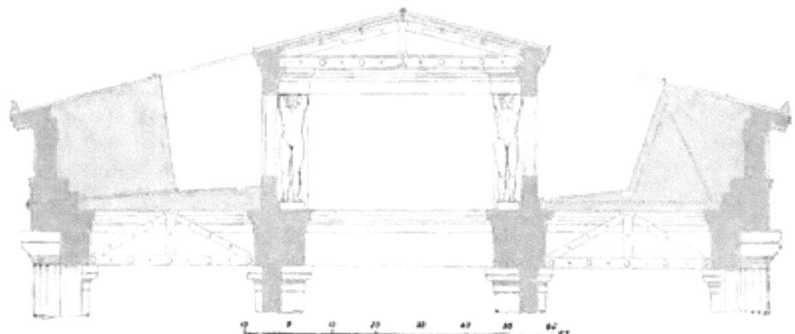
47.—SECTION OF ROOF OF GREAT TEMPLE AT AGRIGENTUM.

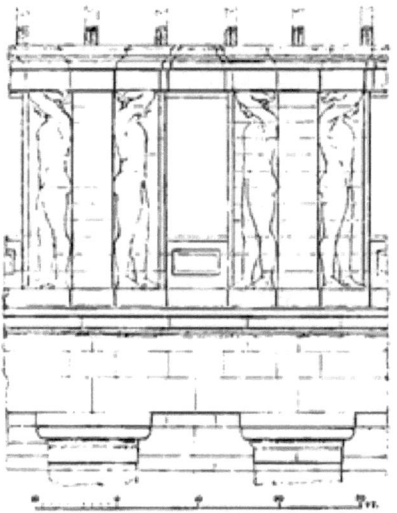
48.—ELEVATION OF UPPER PART OF CELLA WALLS, AGRIGENTUM.

below. But, however this was managed, the light seems certainly to have been introduced through this attic, and the manner in which it was done was the one redeeming feature of this strange temple.

In the diagram of the section of the roof, woodcut No. 47, I have shown two different modes in which the drainage of the opaion might be effected. On the left hand side it is represented as draining towards the exterior through the face of the architrave, which is here built up of small stones. On the right hand, it is represented as conducted by pipes or other mechanical means to the floor of the aisles. In a temple, properly so called, this might be inadmissible, but to an ambulatory or promenade, as this seems to have been, it might have been unobjectionable, and has conveniences which might lead to its adoption. Whichever mode was adopted it seems quite certain that, like all temples, the mode of lighting was through vertical—never through horizontal openings. In the aisles by honest windows, such as we should introduce in our buildings: in the hieron, by a clerestory, like that used in Gothic churches.

There thus seems no doubt—barring the details of construction—about the mode of lighting this great temple at Agrigentum; but the same cannot be said of the sister temple at Selinus, which is another of the six giant temples that the Greeks erected in the great age. It apparently was shaken down by an earthquake, and the remains now lie heaped together on its platform in such confusion that it is almost impossible to make out a plan correctly. In 1830 Messrs. Hittorff and Zanth spent considerable time, and ran great risks, in order to explore them thoroughly, but they had not the means of removing any of the ruins, so that even their plan cannot be quite relied upon. Still less can that of Duca di Serra di Falco,[1] who did not devote the same amount of labour to this investigation. In 1870 M. Hittorff devoted eighteen of the plates[2] of his great work to an elucidation of the plan thus obtained of the temple, and the restoration of it, according to his views. Yet it is easy to see, notwithstanding all the pains that have been bestowed upon it, and the beauty of the plates, it is very far indeed from being satisfactory. In the first place he represents the pronaos as a hall 60 feet by 80 feet, covered with a flat ceiling, without any support;

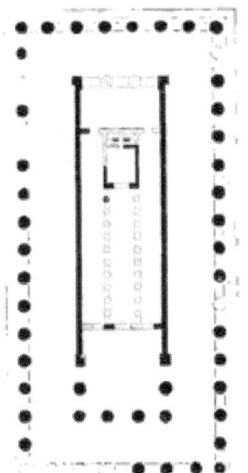

GREAT TEMPLE AT SELINUS. (From Hittorff, Scale 100 ft. = 1 in.)

---

[1] Antichità di Sicilia, vol. ii. pl. xxi.   [2] Architecture Antique de la Sicile, pls. lxii. to lxxix.

but, if I understand him correctly, loaded with lacunaria in stone, which must enormously have increased the difficulty of construction. My impression is, that the Greeks, at the time that the plan of the temple was determined upon, were incapable of constructing such a roof. The Romans in their basilicas might have accomplished it, but only with a lavish use of iron, and more skill in carpentry than the Greeks professed to have. In the state of the mechanical arts at that time I do not believe it would have been attempted. We have just seen that at Agrigentum they hesitated to construct a roof of 45 feet span, and did not carry it out; 60 feet I believe to have been beyond their means.

The arrangement of the cella is even more unsatisfactory. M. Hittorff adopts almost literally my proposal of three tiers of columns, and the light admitted through the third—though with very scant acknowledgment of my priority in proposing it (page 497)—but he places the whole under a perfectly open hypæthron, so that every drop of rain that fell over an area of 60 feet by 160 must have fallen into the temple. As no system of drainage existed anywhere in the temple, in the torrential rains that sometimes occur in that climate, the temple must have been flooded to a most inconvenient extent. It was not thus, I conceive, that the Greeks ever built their temples.

My reading of the riddle is different, suggested by what happened at Mousta, in the neighbouring island of Malta, within the last few years. In 1812 the inhabitants, becoming rich and prosperous under British rule, determined to rebuild their parish church. Instead, however, of pulling it down at once and erecting another in its place, they proposed to construct the new one on such a scale, and with a dome of sufficient height to enclose and cover the old one without in any way interfering with it. By this means the service was continued without interruption till 1860, when the priest was enabled to announce from the altar that the new one was complete, and before the following Sunday the old church was cleared away, and service performed at the same altar as the villagers had always worshipped at under a dome 124 feet in diameter and 160 feet in height—barring details—one of the finest and most remarkable churches in Europe.[1]

My impression is that something of the same sort occurred at Selinus. There seems to have been an old and venerated fane there, apparently an ordinary hexastyle, to which, the arrangement in the cella of small columns three tiers in height, would have been perfectly appropriate. At some period—apparently very early—the Selinuntines seem to have been fired with the ambition of emulating the glories of the Ephesian fane, and commenced the erection of an octastyle peristyle, on the same scale. Whether they ever intended that it should be dipteral instead of pseudo-dipteral, as it now is, is not quite clear; but it can hardly be doubted that when the peristylar arrangements were complete—they never were—the internal disposition of the temple would have been altered to

---

[1] For details of the building, &c., see my History of Architecture, vol. iv. p. 54. 57.

something more in accordance with its magnificence. The bathos of the present insignificant cella arrangements combined with the gigantic exterior could never have been a Greek design. Probably it was intended to substitute a vaulted wooden roof with an hypæthron like that I have proposed for the temple at Ephesus, or that of Jupiter Olympius at Athens, as shown in Plate I. If any one, or any Government—for I fear it is beyond the means of any individual—would undertake to remove the mass of debris that now encumbers the platform on which the temple once stood, its plan might easily be recovered. I fear, however, that it would scarcely repay the trouble and expense. The temple was not finished—or, at least, was in course of reconstruction, probably on quite a new plan—when it was shaken down by an earthquake, and its remains would consequently hardly tell us what it was ultimately intended to have been. Besides this, except for its claim to be one of the six great temples which the Greeks built in their great age, I fear it has no claim on our admiration.

The Temple of Ceres at Eleusis, though architecturally one of the worst, is from an archaeological point of view one of the most interesting of all those that have come down to us from the great age of Greece. It is therefore much to be regretted that our information regarding its remains is so imperfect as it is. Excavations are now in progress on the site, and it consequently requires considerable courage to propound any theories regarding its disposition, which may be considerably modified by facts discovered in the course of these investigations.

In 1797, the party of explorers sent by the Society of Dilettanti to examine the ruins in Asia Minor stopped at Eleusis and made a sketch-plan of the building.[1] It was then, however, as now, concealed by the houses of the modern village; and as they had no means of removing these, or excavating, their plan was of little value. The party sent by the same society under Sir W. Gell in 1817 were more fortunate. They were enabled to make an accurate plan of the temple area and its surroundings, and to make some excavations, by which the dimensions of the temple itself and its portico were ascertained, and also approximately the position of three[2] of its internal pillars. From these details T. P. Gandy published a restoration of the temple, which is one of the most unfortunate attempts of the class that ever was perpetrated by any architect. Artistically it was impossible that the Greeks should have placed a range of columns in front of and in the axis of the doorway. Worse than this, the transverse roof he suggested, 65 feet span, was beyond the means of Greeks to construct. It fades away to nothing at either end, so that even at the present day we could not execute it in wood, and hardly in iron, and how it was to terminate architecturally he seems never to have considered.[3]

---

[1] Antiquities of Ionia, vol. ii. pl. xix.
[2] Unedited Antiquities of Attica, chap. iv. pls. i. to iv.
[3] It is a curious illustration of the utter in-

Scant though the materials are for attempting a restoration of this temple, they are sufficient to enable us to make out the main features with very tolerable certainty. The central pillar of the Dilettanti surveyors is exactly what we might have expected them to find. In the Parthenon, and at Bassæ, a central pillar was placed in a similar position, and the other two pillars found show that a central nave, 40 feet in width from centre to centre of the columns, runs from it to the front entrance right across the temple. The remaining thirty-four columns were then disposed on either hand in the manner indicated in the plan.¹

What we know of this temple is principally derived from a passage in Plutarch, who tells us: "The mystic temple of Eleusis was begun to be built by Coræbus, who proceeded so far as to erect the lower columns and the epistylia. At his death Metagenes of Xypetis added the galleries and the upper columns; Xenocles, the Cholargian, constructed the roof of the opaion over the sanctuary."² The only word doubtful here is "ἀνακτόρου," which I have translated sanctuary. It may be simply "centre," "principal part," but this is of the least possible consequence. The opaion was simply the clerestory, or central range of metopes, by which all the temples of the Greeks were lighted, and this one in no way differed from the others. Vitruvius, on the other hand, tells us that the cella of this temple, "immani magnitudine," was designed by Ictinus, the architect of the Parthenon, but without the portico, which was afterwards added under Demetrius Phalerus, by Philon."³ All this adds to its interest, as connecting it with the great age of Athenian architecture; and the probability is that, the same architect being employed on both buildings, adopted practically the same mode here of lighting that was employed in the Parthenon, and consequently, whatever theory we may adopt for the one temple adds to the probability of its being employed in the other also.

Another point of very great interest connected with the temple is the connexion between the rites celebrated in it with those of the Egyptian Isis, and

---

difference towards these studies that pervades in this country, that no one has ever thought of questioning this impossible restoration. When I proposed one in 1848 (True Principles of Beauty in Art, woodcut 91) which not only could be carried out, but met all the written exigencies of the case, it was totally disregarded, and people go on quoting Mr. Gandy's plan as if it were unquestionable.

¹ If the position of the second row of columns was correctly ascertained, which is doubtful, and they were all equally spaced, the interior of the temple must have been nearly 179 ft. instead of 167. The width of the wall between the portico and the nave was not ascertained. It may have been 5 instead of 10 ft., and there is nothing to show that the front gallery—I presume there was one—may not have been 20 ft. instead of 25.

² Plutarch, vita Pericles: Τὸ δ' ἐν Ἐλευσῖνι τελεστήριον ἤρξατο μὲν Κόροιβος οἰκοδομεῖν καὶ τοὺς ἐν' ἐδάφους κίονας ἔθηκεν αὐτὸς καὶ τοῖς ἐπιστυλίοις ἐπέζευξεν· ἀποθανόντος δὲ τούτου Μεταγένης ὁ Ξυπέτιος τὸ διάζωμα καὶ τοὺς ἄνω κίονας ἐπέστησε· τὸ δ' ὀπαῖον ἐπὶ τοῦ ἀνακτόρου Ξενοκλῆς ὁ Χολαργεὺς ἐκορύφωσε.

³ Vitruvius, præf. vii.: "Eleusine Cereris et Proserpinæ cellam immani magnitudine Ictinus Dorico more sine exterioribus columnis ad laxamentum usus sacrificiorum pertexuit. Eam autem postea, cum Demetrius Phalereus Athenis rerum potiretur Philon, ante Templum in fronte columnas constitutis prostylon fecit."

the consequent similarity of its arrangements with those of Egyptian architecture. The following quotation may state the case a little too strongly, but, on the whole, it expresses nearly the truth : " Les mystères de Cérès suivant Lactance sont

50.—SECTION OF CENTRAL PORTION OF GREAT HALL AT KARNAC.

presque semblables à ceux d'Isis: la Cérès attique est la même divinité que l'Isis Égyptienne (Herod. ii. 59) et cette dernière était la seule en Égypte que du

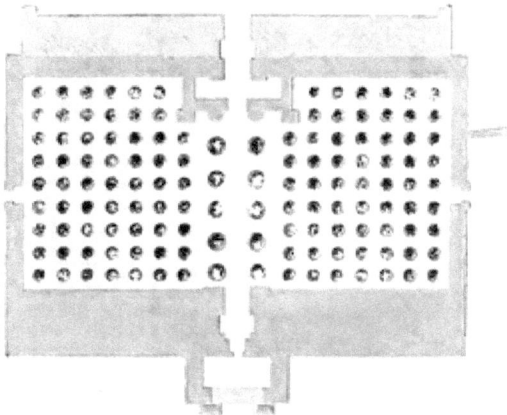

51.—PLAN OF HYPOSTYLE HALL AT KARNAC.

temps d'Hérodote eut des mystères. C'est donc de ces mystères d'Isis que l'on doit déduire en partie ceux de Cérès" (' Essai sur les Mystères d'Eleusis,' p. 9).[1]

[1] Antiquities of Attica, p. 19.

Even, however, if the *litera scripta* should not be sufficient to establish the practical identity of Ceres with Isis, the architectural evidence would go far to confirm it, inasmuch as there seems no doubt that this temple at Eleusis is copied from an Egyptian design. Taking the great hall at Karnac, for instance, as an example, it will be seen that the design consists of a phalanx of columns on either

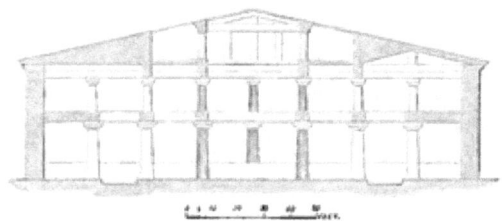

53.—Restored Section of the Temple at Eleusis. (Scale 20 feet to 1 inch.)

hand, separated by an opaion, by which the light is admitted in the same manner to both temples. It is hardly needful to insist on the immense superiority of the Egyptian over the Grecian design. The immense forest of columns supporting a solid stone roof, and the proportions of the central nave to the side aisles, are nearly perfect; while the arrangement of all the columns standing on their solid bases is so infinitely superior to the built-up supports and the wooden roofs of Greek temples, as hardly to admit of comparison from an architectural point of view. Yet the intention is the same in both, though the mode of carrying it out is singularly characteristic of the two styles. The Greeks lavished all their art on the exterior of their temples, in which they produced effects that have never been surpassed; but they seem to have cared less for their interiors, and, except in the case of the Parthenon perhaps, were seldom so successful in them, and singularly unfortunate in this instance. The Egyptians, on the contrary, cared little for their exteriors, archi-

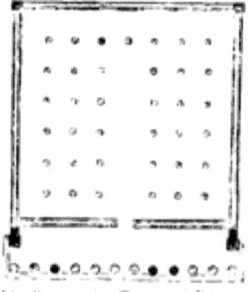

54.—Plan of the Temple at Eleusis. (Scale 100 feet to 1 inch.)

tecturally at least, but lavished all their care on the interior arrangements, and in them have never been surpassed. But barring this essential difference in the mode of treatment, the two designs are as nearly as may be the same. There is also a curious coincidence in dimensions, which can hardly be accidental, the temple being almost exactly one-half of that of the hall, the dimensions of the former being as nearly as could be ascertained 166 or 167 feet square. The hall is a double square of 166 feet, consequently 332 feet in length with an opaion measuring 75 feet across from centre to centre of the columns.[1] According to Vitruvius there is no cella belonging to any Greek temple at all equal to it in size, and, as we know, like it in shape. The most striking difference, and the one which prevents the similarity being obvious at the first glance, arises from the essential difference of the atmospheric circumstances in which the two styles were elaborated. In the rainless climate of Egypt the architects could always employ flat roofs, and their opaions stood out exposed to the full rays of the sun. The Greeks, on the contrary, never could employ flat roofs, but were obliged to give them a sufficient slope to carry off the rain that sometimes fell in torrents in their country. They met this difficulty by counter-sinking them in their roofs, by which they obtained all the advantages of the Egyptian plans, with only the slight difficulty of providing for the drainage of the opening; but this could easily be provided for in fifty ways besides those I have suggested. It would be too absurd to suppose that such men as we know the Greek architects to have been were not equal to meeting a difficulty of this sort. Very inferior men would have conquered it easily.

The one difficulty, however, that occurs in reconstructing the roof of this temple is exactly this one. It is to ascertain how the small quantity of rain that fell in the openings of the opaion were got rid of. It cannot for one moment be supposed that it was allowed to fall fortuitously into the temple, though universally supposed to do so in all restorations hitherto proposed. It is a clumsiness of which it appears to me no Greek architect could possibly be guilty. Nine-tenths of the drainage of this roof is easily accounted for by the expedients already explained, but the remaining tenth is a difficulty. If we could credit the Greeks with the use of a metal or earthenware pipe to convey the water from the roof to the floor, the rest would be easy. The pavement of the temple is 2 feet 2 inches below the level of the portico, and, according to Sir W. Gell's plan, there was a false floor at about 6 feet above the pavement, so that if once brought to the floor it could have been got rid of without difficulty. If, however, the use of such a pipe cannot be admitted, it must have been by such an impluvium as that shown in the woodcut, which for the reasons above stated could have been easily managed. This, however, is just one of those points that the excavation of the ruins, whenever it takes place, will probably clear up, and till it is made it is useless speculating on what will be found. Till then this and many other points must still remain doubtful from the very imperfect data which are now available for their solution.

The Erechtheum at Athens is the only other temple with regard to whose mode of lighting it seems necessary to allude before describing that of the

---

[1] Lepsius, Denkmäler aus Egypten, 1 Abt. pl. 78.

Parthenon. If it were still a moot point whether Greek temples were, or were not, lighted by vertical openings, it would be a most interesting one to insist upon, but after what has been said above, any one who has still any doubts on the subject, had better shut the book before going any further—neither these temples nor any other will affect his faith, and I would not wish to disturb it.

Boetticher, in his 'Tektonik der Hellenen' (Plate 41), suggests that there was a window on each side of the door to the eastern temple or Erechtheum, and probably he was justified in so doing. It may, however, be contended that an ordinary hyperthyrion would be sufficient to light a cella only 24 feet deep for all ordinary occasions, especially as there was no statue, but only three altars inside it. The principal altar, that of Jupiter, was in the portico, and on all occasions of sacrifice or ceremony the doors might be thrown open, and even in our climate the light would then be more than sufficient. The arrangement of the little temple of Nike Apteros, in its immediate proximity and of the same age, seems to warrant this and even more. In that temple behind a tetrastyle portico of Ionic columns there is nothing but two slender pilasters. The whole of the wall is removed, and the temple quite open or only closed by grilles on each side of the central compartment. There is nothing to show that a similar arrangement was not adopted here, though it is by no means probable that the mode of introducing light was carried to that extent in this instance. It is extremely probable, however, that in smaller Ionic temples, such as that at Priene for instance, the wall on each side of the doorway was pierced by windows of greater or less extent, and the light so introduced, whenever it may have been inconvenient or undesirable to introduce it through the roof in the side walls.[1]

The western half of the Erechtheum, which was occupied by the shrine of Minerva Polias, was larger (35 feet by 32), and therefore required a more careful provision for lighting it. It was, however, so encumbered by screens and permanent furniture connected with the "well," and the various treasuries that it contained, that it did not admit of any simple opaion being introduced—even if such had ever been attempted in any of the smaller class of Ionic temples, which is by no means clear. But as lighting through the roof was consequently neither desirable nor practicable, the Greek architects went to work precisely as we should have done in similar circumstances, and opened three windows in the western wall, which answered the purpose admirably.[2] The

---

[1] For the particulars of the plan and arrangement of this temple the reader is referred to two papers I published in the Sessional Papers of the Royal Institute of British Architects in February 1876, and a supplement published in 1880.

[2] It is curious to observe how antiquaries, who are possessed with a mania for unroofing Greek temples, neglect what appears the most obvious evidence when it conflicts with their theories. Beulé for instance, in his restoration of the temple, takes the roof entirely off the

existence of these three windows in the western wall of the temple is proof positive to any one who will take the trouble of thinking about the matter, or is at all acquainted with the principles on which the Greeks designed their temples, that the apartment they were destined to light had no opening in the roof or any other mode of admitting light. Such windows were amply sufficient for the purpose, and any additional means of lighting would have been a superfluity and an absurdity. They afford also a very strong presumption that the sacred olive-tree was not planted in an apartment where it could not receive the dew and fresh air of heaven, where in fact it could not have lived for many years under any circumstances. But no more need be said about that here. Since Michaelis' and I simultaneously pointed out that the tree was planted outside in the open air of the Pandrosium, this has been generally admitted, and the last excuse for unroofing the temple is removed, and in future the windows may be credited with performing that function for which they are amply sufficient. We have copied the windows and the arrangements of this temple in hundreds of chapels and public buildings, but have found no means of improving them. This seems strange, as since then glass has been invented long ago, which ought to have superseded the designs of those who did not possess that material, but without it had erected buildings so perfect and so perfectly adapted to these purposes. The truth of the matter seems to be that whenever from local or other circumstances it was inexpedient to introduce an opaion with vertical lights in the roof, the Greeks, as at Agrigentum and here, had unhesitatingly recourse to windows similar to those we now use, and always with a satisfactory result, but, so far as we can judge, never with so pleasing or so artistic an effect as was produced by the higher and better protected lights in the roof.

Temple of Minerva Polias (Acropole d'Athènes, vol. ii. p. 248), in order to plant the Sacred Olive there, which he assumes, in contradiction to Forchhammer (Daduchos, Kiel, 1875, pl. viii.), could not grow without light or air, and then assumes that the Greeks inserted these three windows in the western wall to light a court-yard open to the sky! Were the Greeks idiots?

[1] Sessional Papers of the Royal Institute of Brit. Arch. in Feb. 1870.

CHAPTER VI.

THE PARTHENON.

THOUGH the Grecian is very far from being a fashionable style of architecture at the present day, it will probably be admitted by all, who have paid much attention to the subject, that, taking it all in all, the Parthenon is the most perfect specimen of architectural art that has yet been erected in any climate, and at any time, by the hand of man. It cannot, of course, compete, in mere masonic magnificence, with such an example as the great hall at Karnac, the most massive, and at the same time most sublime, of all the architectural creations with which the world has hitherto been adorned. It may also be deficient in that picturesque variety and expression of religious aspirations which charms us in some of our medieval cathedrals, but it seems to occupy a happy medium position between the two. It avoids, on the one hand, the too solid gloom of the hall, and on the other the somewhat unsubstantial brightness of the church. No other building ever attracted to it the sister arts of painting and sculpture in such perfection as are found in the Parthenon. No one combined them with the most perfect architecture into one harmonious whole so completely, so that we hardly know to which art to assign the pre-eminence. The paintings, it is true, have perished, but there is little doubt but that they were originally as perfect as either the sculpture or the architecture, and formed the harmonizing link between the two. The Parthenon may, in fact, be considered as the most perfect expression of the aspirations of the most intellectual and most artistic people the world has ever known, and at the time of their most complete and perfect development.

When Stuart first in 1762 made known the beauties of Athenian architecture to his countrymen, it was felt to be a revelation of something better than they had known before. Up to that time they had been taught to believe in Vignola, Palladio, and the architects of the renaissance, and to admire only the splendour of the Roman arts, in their then unrivalled magnificence. For their sake they had been content to abandon the ruder but far more appropriate styles of their forefathers, but when the glories of Grecian art were made known to them, they seized on them with avidity. Every church, every town hall or jail, even private houses, were adorned with hexastyle and octastyle porticos of Grecian Doric, wholly irrespective of their appropriateness to the purposes to which they were applied, or the climate in which they were erected. No better evidence could be afforded of the impression the beauty of the style made on us—though something, it must be confessed, may be ascribed to our own poverty of invention, which makes us ready to copy anything that will save ourselves the trouble of thinking. Although, therefore, we may infer from its universal adoption that we really *felt* the beauty of the style, it cannot be said that we understood exactly in what its superiority consisted, till the publication of Mr. Penrose's book in 1851. He was the first to put before us in a scientific manner the principles that guided the architects in the design of this building. But even now that it is pointed out to us, our eyes do not see, in a newly-erected portico, the want of those delicate curves which were indispensable conditions to the more educated eyes of the Athenians. The delicate hyperbolas and parabolas, which governed the setting out of the moulding and the entasis of the columns, are refinements in masonry which we do not want, and their replacement by curves of a lower order is to us no appreciable defect. So, too, the system of simple ratios which governed the proportion of every part of the design to all the others, was never found anywhere except in Doric temples of this age, and nowhere so perfectly as in the Parthenon. It may be that from its ruined state we are unable to perceive these refinements, but no one with any cultivated feeling for beauty in art ever contemplated the Parthenon even in its decay, without feeling that there was something about it which is seen nowhere else, and which conveys to the mind an impression of its perfection to an extent no other building ever approached.[1]

It is sad to think that less than two hundred years ago this noble building was in all essential respects practically as entire as the Theseion. After surviving the wars and revolutions of more than two thousand years, and even a change of faith, none of its beauties, externally at least, were destroyed. The sculpture of its pediments was still *in situ*, and very little injured. The metopes were all in their places, and its frieze was still complete and perfect in all its parts, and except for the removal of the four at least inner columns of the eastern pronaos to make room for the Christian apse, no injury was done to the exterior. We might consequently have admired this most perfect work of the Grecian architects in all its proportions, and studied the effects they sought with such infinite pains to produce, without any effort of the imagination. It was not till 1687

---

[1] In the following pages no attempt will be made to describe or illustrate those refinements of art as displayed in the Parthenon. This has been so fully and so well done, and with such a wealth of illustration, by Mr. Penrose in his 'Principles of Athenian Architecture,' published by the Dilettanti Society in 1851, that any attempt to explain these principles in a volume like the present would be a work of supererogation, impossible to carry out satisfactorily, nor is it needed. In no instance does it go over the same ground, and may in fact be considered, if anything, complementary to it.

The curves were first noticed, or at least first scientifically investigated, by Mr. John Pennethorne in visits to Athens in 1836-37. He published a magnificent work on the subject in 1878 entitled 'Geometry and Optics of Ancient Architecture,' which is full of interesting speculations on the subject, but does not supersede Mr. Penrose's work, in so far at least as this special temple is concerned.

that a bomb from Morosini's batteries fell accidentally into a magazine of powder which the Turks had stored in the temple, and reduced the whole to the state of ruin in which we now find it.[1] Enough, however, is still left to enable the careful student to recover the exact plan, and to restore the external form of the temple with perfect exactitude, and to the "mind's eye" to reproduce its beauties. What we lament is, that we cannot without an effort revel in the contemplation of this masterpiece of art, which has so narrowly escaped being handed down perfect to the present time.

It is not so clear whether this catastrophe of 1687 was as fatal to our knowledge of the design of the interior as it was to the effect of the exterior. Long ages

[1] The place where the bomb fell can still be traced on the pavement by its ruined state, under where the central dome existed, a little nearer the apse of the Christian church.

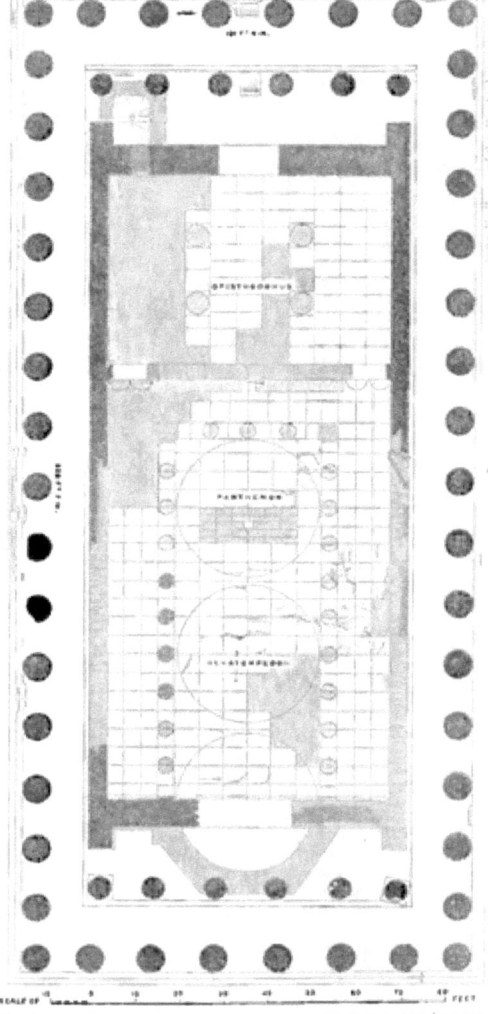

51.—PLAN OF PARTHENON IN ITS PRESENT STATE, BUT SHOWING THE REMAINS OF THE CHRISTIAN CHURCH.

before it occurred the temple had been converted into a church, and extensive internal alterations been introduced in consequence to suit it for its new destination, without this, however, affecting the exterior. It is not known when this conversion took place, but it must have been early, before all veneration for the beauties of classical art had quite died out. Had the iconoclastic mania then prevailed, as it did after Justinian's time, they never would have left its Pagan sculptures so complete and uninjured, as they were found even at the beginning of this century. It probably was between the age of Constantine and that of Justinian that it occurred, but there seems no means available for ascertaining this.

No extensive alterations in plan were necessary to suit the temple to its new destination, and on the whole those that were introduced seem to have been judicious—if one dare say so—improvements. The first was to make the western the principal entrance instead of the eastern, which, from its situation towards the Propylæa, it naturally was. This being done, the next change was to turn the opisthodomos of the temple into the pronaos or narthex of the church, which was a decided improvement. In ancient times a treasury was indispensable, and for this purpose about one-third of the temple was cut off and separated entirely from the naos. By throwing the whole into the church the Christians certainly utilized the area in a better manner, and produced a finer interior, in plan, than was possible under the original arrangement. The change was effected by cutting a central doorway through the screen wall that separated the two parts of the temple, while probably retaining also the two lateral ones, that seem to have existed as part of the original building.[1] To complete the change the central pillar, which supported the gallery, was removed, and replaced by an arch. But the greatest change was to close the original eastern entrance, and replace it by an apse, the foundations of which can yet be traced, of the same diameter as that of the three domes which replaced the original roof.

When Spon and Wheeler visited Athens in 1676[2] they describe these arrangements as complete. Three of the Ionic pillars (they do not mention them) that supported the roof of the opisthodomos were still standing, but the fourth, which from some cause had become ruined, the Kislar Aga had replaced by a pier of rude masonry. They describe also with minute accuracy the arrangement of the pillars of the nave, twenty on the ground floor supporting a gallery, and twenty-one on the upper, which is exactly the number we infer from the marks now remaining on the floor. But what excited their attention most was the roof, composed of (three) domes, as marked in faint lines on the plan, so arranged as to exclude the light almost entirely from the church. This is one of the reasons for thinking it probable that the conversion took place before the time of Justinian. After the erection of St. Sophia, all the Byzantine domes we know of had a circle

---

[1] Boetticher, Untersuchungen auf der Acropolis, p. 151, fig. 34 & 35.
[2] Jacob Spon's Voyage d'Italie &c., fait és Années 1675 et 1676, Lyon, 1678. George Wheeler's Journey over Greece, London, 1682.

of windows immediately above the springing of the dome. The Roman ones, on the contrary, were all dark, as these were; their buildings—except the Pantheon—depending on windows in the side walls for the light they required. Had it been desired, nothing would have been easier than to have introduced lights where they were wanted, only that the domes must then have formed a real roof. Here, as in our mediæval Domical churches, they were under a wooden roof, and not seen externally. Granting this, nothing seems so natural as the application of a roof of domes to this temple. The old wooden roof was probably decayed, plundered of its bronze ornaments, and it would have required more skill than, we may suppose, the architects of that day possessed to restore it as an ornamental covering to a Christian church. The cupola, on the contrary, was the natural form the Byzantine roof took, admitting, as it did, of being adorned with paintings and mosaic to an extent which in any other form was impossible.[1] If, as we suppose, the under and upper ranges of columns were buttressed first by the gallery floor, and then by the stone roof of the opaion, nothing could have been easier than the construction in wood and plaster of these domes. There is height enough below the external roof to have made them semicircular, but it is more probable they were, as most domes of that age, either segmental or elliptical. Barring the deficiency of light consequent on the substitution of these opaque domes for the original clerestory, the Christians must by these alterations have produced a very beautiful and commodious church, though it is one the loss of which we can hardly regret. As in the Theseion, they had entirely obliterated all trace of the original roof, and by their tunnel vault in that temple, and their domes here, prevented us from having any material evidence of the original arrangement, a fragment of which would have been more valuable to us than all the Christians effected in their adaptations.[2]

---

[1] In alcuni luoghi per ornamento vi erano alcune cupole le di cui estremità si componevano, di mattoni à musaico. In una di queste cupole cadde la Bomba, mentre nel pavimento superiore sarebbe stata vana, di tal contrasto veruno essendo in potentissimo tempera formato. Ant. Balbigne, Lettere Memorabili, Raccolta II., Lalande II. 187, quoted by Stuart, p. 11. by Michaelis, p. 347.

[2] Fifty years ago the celebrated German architect, Klenze, had an opportunity of reproducing the Parthenon in fac-simile, which is not likely to occur again in our day. In 1830 he was commissioned by King Louis of Bavaria to build the Walhalla, a temple dedicated to the glory of Germany and all Germans who had rendered their country illustrious by deeds or words. The Parthenon was chosen as the model, and it was copied, as nearly as may be, in detail and dimensions, barring some slight modifications in the latter, the motive of which it is difficult to understand. These, however, are trifles compared with a painful mistake which was made in placing it in so lofty a stylobate, that its apparent dimensions are diminished so as to lose half their effect. Barring this mistake, which no Greek would have made, he had no difficulty with the exterior. Enough remains at Athens to enable any one to copy this exactly. When, however, he turned to the interior, instead of attempting to reproduce the design of Ictinus, he threw it entirely aside and made a new design of his own. This, though rich in marble and metal work, to an extent hardly known in modern times—it is said to have cost more than a million sterling—may safely be pronounced an entire failure.

He arranged the interior as one great hall

In consequence of the temple being first turned into a church, and then entirely gutted by the explosion of 1687, there are few material remains to guide us to a restoration of the interior. But though few, they are not the less certain and important. On the floor of the cella there are the marks of the bases of at least seven columns, which can be distinctly traced. The diameter has been ascertained with perfect certainty as 3·656 feet from fillet to fillet, and comparing that with the external columns, 6·45, it gives a height as nearly as may be of 19 feet. Even this, however, is far from absolute, as it is by no means clear that the Greeks may not have used a more slender proportion for the columns in the interior than in those of the exterior of their temples. They did so at Bassæ,

with a small opisthodomos, containing the staircases to the galleries. The hall he divided into three compartments by two piers projecting forward so as to reduce the central space to 40 Bavarian feet. On these piers rest two massive trusses which divide the roof into three compartments, and in each of these he placed an enormous skylight of ground glass; the skylight and the whole framing of the roof being supported by a most elaborate construction of wrought iron. This is concealed of course, but the whole effect of these skylights, both internally and externally, is most unpleasing, and as unlike anything a Grecian architect ever did or would have done as well can be conceived.

If instead of this, he had only set himself to study the interior as well as the exterior by merely rearranging the parts as shown in the annexed woodcut, he might have produced an interior worthy of the best age of Greek art. In the diagram the architectural arrangements are identical with those of the original temple; their use and orientation only is changed, but curiously enough only to the extent to which the early Christians had altered them when they took possession of the Parthenon.

Should it ever occur to any Scotch millionaire to complete the national monument commenced on the Calton Hill in Edinburgh, he will, with these slight modifications in plan, now be able to reproduce the interior of that celebrated temple exactly, or at least as nearly as this or any subsequent investigation may determine. A colossal statue of Britannia would appropriately replace that of Minerva in the place indicated, and there is ample room for any number of statues and busts, or inscriptions. The statues would appropriately occupy the vestibule, which of course would be, in that case, lighted by an opaion, which could easily be introduced. Instead of two windows in the clerestory on each side being opened to the

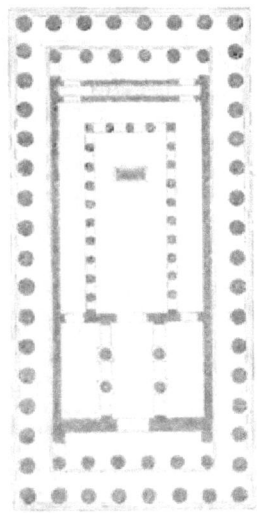

Diagram of suggested rearrangement of the interior of the Parthenon.

direct rays of the sun, as I suppose was the case at Athens, five probably out of the nine would require to be glazed in the climate of Edinburgh, but this would be no difficulty or defect either internally or externally.

probably did so at Olympia, and may have done so here. But leaving this to be settled hereafter, I have drawn the upper range of columns as 11 feet 6 inches, which is certainly in excess of what the examples at Pæstum and Ægina would lead us to expect. There the upper are only half the height of the lower columns, and even when we regard the two columns as forming part of one cone, it may be a little too tall. I have made it so, however, because there is a gallery here, while there is not in either of the two instances named; and that may have required a stouter column below, and more head room above to meet the artistic requirements of the case. With these adjustments, the total height of the two orders only reaches to between 36 and 37 feet.[1] A foot may be added or taken away from the dimensions, but beyond that limit I do not conceive they can be stretched. There thus remains a space of at least 10 or 12 feet before the line is reached of any roof that can be put over this part; and if this space was not used as a clerestory to admit light to the interior, as shown in the section (Plate III.), it is difficult to understand how it was employed.[2]

In ornamenting this clerestory I have introduced columns of the Corinthian order, copied from those of the Temple of the Winds. There is no authority for this, but I know of no order that would go so well with the Doric; it seems most appropriate for the purpose for which it is here used. The order has no base, and the capital is simpler and more solid than any example of the order that remains to us.[3] A third Doric order, it appears to me, would be monotonous and unmeaning, and if this Corinthian order is not admitted, I would prefer square piers and pilasters, as I proposed in my original design.

In plan, the interior of the Parthenon was divided into two principal apartments, the opisthodomos and the hekatompedon. The former occupied nearly one-third of the whole length, including the thickness of the division wall, or 46 feet 10 inches, as compared with 98 feet. Its roof was supported by four

---

[1] Hittorff and others who wish to treat these columns as supporting the roof, which is a necessary condition of their mode of lighting by a hole in the roof, make these dimensions 25 ft. for the lower order, 15 ft. for the upper, and 46 ft. for the total of the two orders. These dimensions I conceive to be totally inadmissible on any doctrine of proportion, or from any authority derived from any existing examples.

[2] While this work was in progress I have had an opportunity of experimenting on a full-sized scale on this mode of lighting, though with details adapted to this climate. Miss North's Gallery at Kew is constructed with an opaion similar to that of the Parthenon but arranged so as to light a collection of pictures instead of a statue. The experiment has been perfectly successful. There is not, so far as I know, a better lighted gallery in England for the purpose for which it was designed.

[3] There have been frequent reports of Corinthian capitals found in and about the Parthenon (Penrose, footnote p. 5). Inwood found a fragment of one, which he restored and engraved, pl. 22, and other examples have been found. But none of these seem to have any bearing on the question. The baldacchino of the Christian church was supported by four Corinthian pillars, and others may have been introduced in other places, and were probably ancient examples, but there is no proof that any of them were employed in the construction of the original temple.

Ionic columns, which are entirely gone, though their position on the floor is indicated with certainty. In all the earlier representations of the temple six pillars are introduced, but the error arose apparently from a clumsiness in the description of Sir Geo. Wheeler, which led to what he said regarding the six inner columns of the posticum being mistaken for those of what he supposed to have been the pronaos.[1]

It does not appear that any light was introduced into this apartment through the roof, though it would have been easy to do so if the architect had so wished. The pillars are 17 feet apart from centre to centre, and if an opaion had been introduced between the central ones on either side, it would have thrown a flood of light into the apartment, more perhaps than was thought necessary. As it was only used as a treasury, sufficient light was introduced through the doorway to illuminate for all the uses it was put to. This doorway was of the extraordinary height of 33 feet, with a width of only 14, so that the whole of the upper half might without any disproportion be fitted with a grating, or hyperthyrion, which would admit all the light that was required for its use as a treasury. No works of art were apparently exhibited there.

In 1862 Herr Boetticher[2] discovered distinct traces of two doorways leading from the opisthodomos to the hekatompedon. These were about 5 feet in width, and were closed by bronze doors in two valves, the marks of which were distinctly traceable on the pavement. They are situated, not exactly in the centre of the side aisles, but are pushed towards the side walls, as nearly as they could be placed, to admit of the valves being folded back against the wall in which they were placed, without interfering with the outer walls on the one hand, and the foot of the stairs on the other. It is probable that there were other doors—probably in wood—on the side of the opisthodomos, and that the locks of these were under the control of the treasurers of the opisthodomos, while the keys of the bronze ones were in the possession of the priests of the temple.

The cella, or interior apartment, was called in ancient times by the Greeks the hekatompedon, or the "hundred footed," though it does not merit that appellation when measured by the high standard we are accustomed to find in Parthenon measurements. According to Penrose's plan (Plate 4), it measures 98·04 English feet, as compared with 101·361, which is the length of the upper step of the portico, which was stated and found to be exactly 100 Greek feet. It is therefore more than 3 feet short of the required quantity. It is true, Mr. Watkiss Lloyd, who has paid especial attention to the subject, suggests that the measurement must be taken from the *face* of the western wall to the *centre* of the eastern one—measured, of course, in the doorway—but this is so anomalous

---

[1] Sir Geo. Wheeler's Journey into Greece. London, 1682, p. 362.
[2] Untersuchungen auf der Akropolis zu Athen, p. 165, fig. 34, 35.

a way of measuring an apartment that it can hardly be admitted, though by that means we obtain the required dimension.

A more probable suggestion is that the cella was set out in the proportion of 3 to 2, with a modulus of 32 Greek feet. But even this falls short by about 2 feet 8 inches from the truth in the length, and about 1 foot in the breadth; but it was apparently thought sufficiently near for constructive purposes in the interior, where no principle was involved.

According to this theory, the length of the cella was made three of these moduli, 96 feet (97·4 English), while two were allotted to the width. This last dimension was again approximately subdivided, one modulus (32·233 feet) being given to the centre aisle, and one-half (15·365) to each of the side aisles. These dimensions are so nearly true, and form so beautiful a proportion, that we may safely assume that it was on some such scheme that the interior was set out, though, if it was so, it is strange that it does not agree more nearly with the actual dimensions than it does.

Whether this was the proportionate scale adopted or not, we know that the hekatompedon was divided into two parts, one of which was called the Parthenon proper, because, apparently, it contained the statue. The marks of a railing about 2 feet in front of the pedestal of the statue marked its eastern boundary, and a rail between the pillars probably defined its northern and southern limits. Whether it extended westward to the wall, or was bounded by the pillars there also, there is nothing to show. Most probably the latter was the case, as it evidently was the most sacred part of the temple; and if I am right in placing the stairs where I have done, it is scarcely probable that they would be included in the sanctuary.

Strange to say, there has not been discovered any paragraph in any ancient author that tells us how the roofs of Greek temples were constructed; and except the often quoted expression of Strabo, κορυφὴ τῆς ὀροφῆς, "the summit of the roof," there is none that even indirectly hint how it was done. That they were in wood, covered externally with tiles, either in earthenware or marble, is, of course, clear enough; but as no vestige of the woodwork, by which the tiles were sustained, now remains, we are left very much to our conjectures as to details. Still, however, on a review of the whole evidence, there can be little hesitation in affirming that the whole of the woodwork used in the construction of these roofs was displayed as completely and as truthfully as in our best mediæval roofs, and with as pleasing an effect. Naturally from our habit of imitating Grecian roofs in plaster, our first idea is that their temples were covered with flat ceilings. Those, however, which are so constructed are copied from the details of the lacunaria of the pteronata of the peristyle of temples which were so narrow that they could be roofed with single stones; but the cellas were seldom so narrow that this system could be applied to them. Even if it had been possible internally, it would have been inapplicable, for in a rainy climate like that of Greece the roof must have been constructed with a slope to carry off the moisture. In Egypt it was appropriate, but therein lies the essential difference in the two styles.

It was not done even in so small a temple as that at Bassæ (ante, p. 79), though there the cella was so narrow that it was possible to construct a roof over it entirely of stone. But even if attempted there, it must have followed the lines of the external roof, as shown in Plate II. It was not, however, because, as already explained, it would have involved a copy of wooden construction in stone, which would have been contrary to the true principles of Greek art. It was in accordance with them that reminiscences of wooden construction should be employed in architectural decoration as mere ornaments, but it is quite a different thing to repeat a wooden form as an essential part of the construction of any building. From an attentive study of the roof at Bassæ, we gather that the rafters were in wood, even when the under side of the marble tiles was seen, and à fortiori we infer that the timbers of the roof of the Parthenon were an important feature in the decoration, when the tiles were laid on a planking of cedar, or at least some internal framing of timber, which prevented them being visible from below.

It may, however, be suggested that if a flat stone ceiling was impossible, there may have been one in wooden pannels. To this, of course, there is no constructive objection, but the artistic one seems almost insuperable. An open roof, as shown in Plates III. and IV., would have been infinitely more beautiful, and in this instance far more appropriate. The chryselephantine statue of Minerva, which this temple was erected to enshrine, was, as we learn from Pliny, 26 cubits in height, or nearly 40 feet.[1] If it had been a detached statue placed on a pedestal, as we are in the habit of treating statues which we consider only as curiosities, even this might not represent the whole height, and we might have to add that of the pedestal to the 26 cubits. Looking, however, at the sculptures of the base, with its sphinx, and the serpent, and all its other ornaments, these seem so essentially an integral part of the whole composition, that the only fair interpretation of the passage in Pliny seems to be that the height he mentions applied to the whole composition, measured from the pavement of the temple to the crest of the helmet on the image of the goddess.

As the temple is only 56 feet in height to the summit of the roof externally, and 3 to 4 feet must be allowed for the thickness of the tiles and the planking that supported them, with the necessary framing, it is of the utmost importance to have an open space of 12 or 13 feet above the head of the statue. Not only does this prevent any idea of the statue appearing too large for its situation, but the framing takes away from feeling that superincumbent weight might crush the statue as it stands. With a flat ceiling, however strongly framed, this would almost inevitably be the case, if placed only 6 or 7 feet above its head.

---

[1] Pliny, lib. xxxvi. ch. v. p. 652.

By the adoption of a roof of open framework these inconveniences are avoided, and the statue forms a pleasing part in a framework which seems in every respect appropriate to it.

Another advantage of this arrangement is that it admits of the peplos being suspended above the head of the goddess in a manner which could hardly be effected with any solid ceiling. If the temple had a flat roof of any sort, the peplos being made as a canopy would have been impossible; but draped from the timbers of an open roof it becomes not only appropriate but beautiful. The form which I conceive the framing took is a development of the early timber roof described in a previous chapter (*ante*, p. 59). In designing a roof for the Parthenon we are bound to bear in mind the original form which open timber roofs exhibited in the early temples of the Greeks. The conservative spirit which characterized all they did never would have neglected these earlier suggestions; but the perfected arts of the time demanded that they should be used with all the elegance which the art of the day demanded. The main features of the design thus became clear enough; but whether the drawings represent the roof as actually carried out must be determined hereafter. It is probably more like it than anything that has yet been attempted.

Flat ceilings in either wood or plaster were unknown—so far as I know—in classical times. In stone they were impossible, till the Romans adopted the plan of vaulting them, which the Greeks never attempted, in stone at least, though they may have occasionally employed curvilinear roofs in wood, in imitation of the more permanent form of constructions. Open timber roofs, on the contrary, seem to have been commonly employed, and were continued down till late on in the Middle Ages, and often with the happiest effects. Not on this side of the Alps, it is true, but in Italy many of the basilicas, and even the smaller churches, derive their principal charm from their continuing this practice of the ancient Greeks.[1] In Greece itself, and in the East generally, they were at an early period superseded by the domes of the Byzantines.

---

[1] It is curious to observe when attentively considered how little change the early Christians made in the internal arrangements of the classical temples and basilicas. They purposely avoided copying their exteriors, for the purpose of proclaiming their horror for Pagan superstitions, but they did not find it so easy to invent new and convenient interiors as to dispense with their external ornaments. They only modified them so that the imitation should not easily be detected.

This section of the Church of Sta. Agnese at Rome, which was built almost certainly while the Parthenon was still standing in its original Pagan form, is, "mutatis mutandis," an exact copy of it. There is the same lower colonnade, the same gallery, the same clerestory, and the same open roof, though with only eight spaces

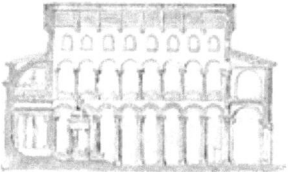

Section of Church of Sta. Agnese, Rome.

As mentioned above, the early Greeks, for obvious reasons, used no iron in the construction of their roofs, though latterly, with more complicated forms of carpentry, iron may have been used in construction, though never apparently in an ornamental form. Bronze, on the contrary, we know was used at as early a time as the erection of the Treasuries of Mycenæ and Orchomenos to a lavish extent, and continued to be employed during all the ages of Greek art, and half the forms of her architectural ornamentation are derived from it. This ornament of a capital, for instance, is not copied from anything in wood or stone, but must have been originally a bronze ornament applied to some earlier capital, which

instead of ten, and arches being naturally introduced instead of flat architraves. The same is true of the Basilica of San Lorenzo fuori le Mura, which presents the same features, and being constructed in part with ancient fragments, is at first sight more like a classical interior, though it is not in reality. The stone grilles in the windows are perhaps a more distinct reminiscence of the bronze screens that were everywhere used in classical clerestories, than anything found in Sta. Agnese.

It would require more space and many more

52. — SAN LORENZO FUORI LE MURA, ROME. (From Lenoir.)

illustrations than are appropriate to this work to show how the interval was bridged over, and how the Pagan gradually faded into the Christian styles. In other circumstances it might be worth while attempting it, as the investigation would throw considerable light both on what took place before and what occurred after the period of transition. But this is not the place to attempt it. All that is required here is to indicate a path that is sure to lead to the most fertile results when properly explored.

being admired, was added in stone to the next executed examples, and so with many others. The metal was, however, too precious to escape the barbarians who overran Greece in the dark ages, so few examples have reached our time.

ORNAMENT IN IMITATION OF BRONZE, FROM A CAPITAL OF THE TEMPLE OF THE SMINTHIAN APOLLO.
(From the Antiquities of Ionia, vol. iv.)

If challenged, it might be difficult to prove mathematically that bronze was used extensively in the construction or for the decoration of the roof of the Parthenon; but looking on the subject in all its bearings under all the circumstances of the case, it seems a fair inference that this was the case. Whether I have succeeded in reproducing even to a moderate extent the design of lētima is another question,[1] of which others must be the judges, but the principles that must guide any one who makes the attempt appear to be tolerably evident. In the first place he must keep steadily in mind the probable progress of such an invention as the application of bronze for this purpose, and must not be frightened by archaisms if they intrude themselves upon him; but above all, he must look to the high position which all the arts connected with architecture had attained at the time when the Parthenon was built. All the mechanical difficulties had long been conquered, and the architect could play with the decorative features, untrammelled by any constructive difficulties; his object, therefore, was more to accentuate than to express the constructive features of the roof, and to adorn it so as to produce the most pleasing effect from below. My own impression is, that the bronze sockets to receive the ends of the trusses are almost indispensable to connect the architecture of the roof with that of the walls. I think the line of bosses, or shields, at the juncture of the queen posts would have a most pleasing effect, and at the same time carry the apparent metallic supports well towards the centre, where naturally it appears weakest. The great strap at the juncture of the king posts is an important part of the simulated construction, which gives strength and dignity to the whole, and might perhaps be made even more important with good effect. The longitudinal bronze ornaments along the central ridge are suggested by constructural features, used currently at the present day, and may therefore have been used in Greece; but this, as most of the design, must naturally be mere conjecture, and if any one thinks that he can do better, he will serve a good cause by trying. The subject is interesting and worthy of more attention than I have yet been able to bestow upon it. The whole of this bronze work, whatever its form may have been, was most probably relieved by gilding to a very considerable extent, and if the wood-

[1] I have been assisted in my designs for the bronze work of this roof by my friend Mr. H. Stannus, who has paid considerable attention to the subject.

work of the roof were of cedar, or any red pine, the effect of bronze, partly of its natural colour, and partly of a more brilliant yellow, must, it is conceived, have been beautiful in the extreme. Such a roof would have been at least as appropriate as any of the open timber roofs which the mediæval architects designed for our churches and halls—better, indeed, for they were bad carpenters—while the decoration being of the best age of Greek art, would have been infinitely superior to the rude quaintnesses upon which they depended for their adornment. It is a pity its effect is not likely to be tried on a sufficient scale to enable the public to judge in what its beauties or defects really consisted.

Another feature of the design which must have been most important for the general effect, consisted in the grilles or lattice-work with which the windows of the opaion were filled. These were necessary, not only as a partial protection against the weather, but because any blinds or curtains that might have been used to protect the interior against the rain or sun, would by their means be rendered thoroughly effectual for the purpose. Without them they might have been blown inwards or outwards, and in fact be rendered comparatively useless as a protection against the sun or the weather.

There is very little to guide us in the design of these grilles; but I conceive they were extremely rich and elaborate—more so, perhaps, than I have shown them in the drawings, and must have been gilt throughout. This was necessary, not only as the crowning feature of design of excessive richness, but because it was necessary to prevent the irregularity of the openings of the opaion and the portions of the external roof from being perceived from below, which a gilt screen of this sort would perfectly effect.

In the drawings these grilles are carried across the western gallery in front, not only because I consider this indispensable for the general effect of the design, but because by this means an upper gallery would be formed round three sides of the temple, in which the women of the congregation might be placed, and might take part in the festivals without their presence being obtrusively observed by the ministrants. I must leave it to others better acquainted with the social statistics of Greece to say how far this separation of the sexes in temples took place in ancient times. My own impression is, that females, except as performers, were not admitted to take part in the Greek festivals, or did not at least. If this was so, this gallery of the opaion would afford accommodation for a vast number of them, where they would be practically as unseen as our ladies in the gallery set apart for them in the House of Commons.

The only other feature in the design which it is necessary to allude to here is the stairs, which, as in the temple at Olympia, led from the floor to the gallery, and from that to the opaion. These were in this instance certainly in wood, and consequently have disappeared. Had they been in stone they would have been inserted in the thickness of the eastern wall, as at Pæstum, and the temple of Concord at Agrigentum and elsewhere in Sicily. No trace of them, however, is found here, and the only indication of their presence is in the fact that the two doorways leading from the hecatompedon to the opisthodomos are not in the middle of the aisles, but pushed as far on the sides as would enable their double doors to be laid back against the wall. This is so awkward that there must have been a strong motive for it, and the only conceivable one that occurs to me is that it was done to make room for the stairs without making them too steep.[1] Besides this, Boetticher remarked (Fig. 54) at 11 feet from the outer wall that the pavement had been roughed to receive an erection of some sort. So far as can be made out, it appears as if a stone was tailed here more than 1 foot into the transverse wall, and projected on the floor at least 2 feet 8 inches. He did not trace it further, but what he saw would exactly fit the theory that it was placed there to stop the foot of the stairs leading to the gallery. Assuming this, there is just room enough for a flight of steps at an angle of 45°, the usual slope in ancient stairs, to extend to a landing, in the centre of the gallery, on either hand; and, of course, another parallel to it would lead easily from the gallery floor to the opaion.

We have no example to guide us in the design of these stairs, nor of the hand-rail which guarded them on the outside, nor can we tell how far they were supported by pillars or outside framing. A log of wood 30 feet in length does not seem beyond the constructive power of the Greeks, and if that was used no further support was required. But without further examples all these details must be left undetermined. Fortunately they are of very little consequence, as the stairs, from their position, interfered very little with the general design of the interior.

Having worked up these materials to as great an extent as they seemed capable of in drawings, it only remained to try and devise some means by which the effect of this mode of lighting could be practically exemplified. It need hardly be said that no one at the present day has the experience which would enable him to predicate what the effect of these arrangements would be for lighting such a statue as that of the Minerva of the Parthenon. For this purpose a model was made of the cella and adjacent parts, on the scale of one-fortieth of the real size, 3·33 feet to one inch, and a model of the statue to the same scale placed in it. When first constructed the opaion was left open for nearly the whole length of the cella, only the two bays next the door being constructed solidly. The light from this opening, as was to be expected, was found to be excessive, and gradually the opening was closed; till eventually, after studying the effect under all circumstances of light, it was found that a space of about 17 feet wide on each side of the ridge was ample for all purposes.

It was further found by experiment that the proper situation for this opening

---

[1] In the temple at Ægina, the door leading to the posticum is not in the centre, I believe from the same cause.

or skylight was opposite the central bay of the whole eleven spaces into which the nave is divided. By this arrangement four and a half bays are left on either side of the two which receive direct light from the outside. This arrangement got over one of the great difficulties of all previous proposals, for, by restricting the opening to 17 feet, a small pediment would easily throw on either side of it all the rain that might fall on the ridge beyond the opening, and we have thus only to deal with the rain that may fall on a space of 17 feet by 13 feet at the outside, which is so insignificant that it is easily disposed of.

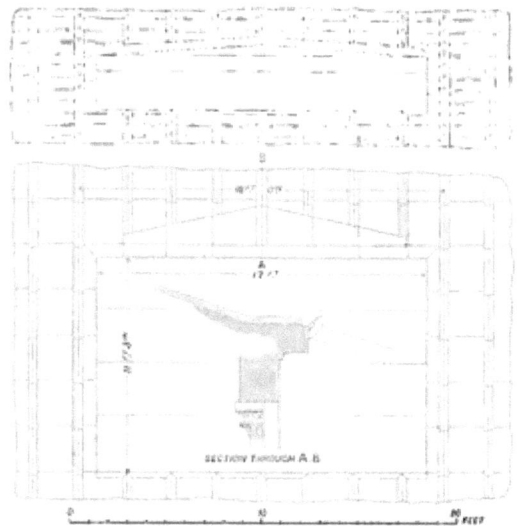

75.—Diagram showing the Plan and Elevation of the Opening of the Roof of the Parthenon.

These openings in the roof externally nowhere correspond exactly with the internal arrangements, and it is vain to try and make them do so, for the internal columns are nowhere exactly opposite the external ones. They are situated nearly—within a very few inches—between the sixth pillar from the east front, and the tenth from the western face of the temple.

In such a temple as that at Bassæ, where the roof could be seen on all sides, this want of exact symmetry would have been intolerable; but in the Acropolis, where the roof of the Parthenon could be nowhere seen, it was of the least possible consequence. The proof that the Athenians thought so, is evident from the arrangement of the tiles, as shown in the annexed woodcut. The position of the acroteria was determined absolutely by that of the triglyphs—one over, and one between each—and consequently they were 3 feet 6 inches apart; but the tiles were only 2 feet 4 inches in width, so that there were three tiles to two acroteria, which could not possibly have happened had they anywhere been visible in conjunction with the columns of the peristyle. While this was the case, the minor defect of want of exact symmetry in the position of the opaion might very well be disregarded, and any attempt to treat it ornamentally would have been quite out of place. In the woodcut (No. 59) I have treated it as plainly as possible.

It would, of course, have been easy to diminish the extent of light by diminishing the height of the opaion, by closing the lower part of it. This was

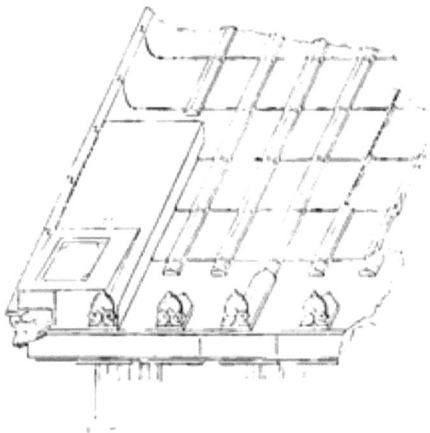

Angle of Roof of Parthenon. (From Penrose, pl. 17.)

no doubt the mode in which it was effected in the smaller temples, where only an internal metope of no great height was employed, and where the light was probably nearly equally diffused along the whole length of the cella. But where, as in this instance, the object was to throw the light on a single statue, it was indispensable that the light should be concentrated on a single point, and this could only be effected by preserving the whole height of the opaion throughout.

Another advantage from this restricted opening is that, while it throws a flood of light on the statue and its surroundings, it does not do so abruptly. The two half bays of the opaion on each side of the central one, which only are exposed to the direct light to the extent of one-half, appear equally lighted throughout from below. The two on either side of them still transmit a considerable volume of light to the interior. Even those beyond them, on the right and left, admit some. Beyond this, at the entrance end, the hyperthyrion, or the open door, would admit light to the floor of the temple, where it was most wanted, but without interfering with the lighting of the statue; while at the inner end of the cella the comparative gloom produced by cutting off the light there is one of the most pleasing effects produced by this mode of lighting. It forms a background to the statue, which is artistically invaluable. If the gilded grille were also extended across it so as to prevent the western wall of the temple from being distinctly seen, except where it was occupied by the stairs, or other permanent furniture, not only would the apparent length be immensely increased, but a brilliant background be afforded for the statue, such as never was provided for such an object in any temple we are acquainted with.

By far the most important result from this mode of construction, and, as it happens, the most satisfactory, is the manner in which the light is thrown on the chryselephantine figure of Minerva itself. Some twenty, or it may be thirty, statues have come down to us from antiquity, all professing to be copies of this celebrated statue; but there is not one of them that fulfils all the required conditions, or that can be quoted as an authority. It is a curious but an undeniable fact, that in an age when art is a true and living expression of men's feelings and aspirations, copying is impossible. Thus the great work of Phidias may have inspired hundreds of men to try and reproduce it, but from this cause they never did so without some alteration which may have appeared to them an improvement, either from the different scale or the different purpose to which the statue was to be employed. Instead, therefore, of relying on these copies, we are reduced, for the restoration of the statue, entirely to verbal descriptions of it. The only one that has been handed down to us by a reliable eye-witness is that of Pausanias, which, though brief, is distinct. It is as follows. After stating that the statue is of gold and ivory, he goes on to say: "The image of Minerva is erect, draped with a garment reaching to her feet, on her breast is a head of Medusa, carved in ivory, as is also a Victory about 4 cubits in height. In her hand she holds a spear, and at her feet lies the shield, and near the spear is a serpent, which is supposed to be Erichthonios. On the base of the statue is represented the birth of Pandora."¹ One hand, either the right or left, was occupied by holding the spear, and the other — it could not be the same — by holding the Victory; but as she had not three hands, either the shield must have rested against her dress, or it must have been supported by the wrist of the hand that held the Victory, as was suggested by Quatremère de Quincy.¹ It is nearly impossible that it should have rested against her side, because both sides of it were most elaborately carved, the inside by the war of the gods and the giants, the outside by the war with the Amazons.² Among the former he introduced his own portrait, and so contrived the entire construction, in some mysterious manner we do not quite comprehend, that if any one attempted to remove it the whole fell to pieces.³ It becomes, however, partially intelligible if we consider that the shield was employed to support the arm of the statue, and also the Victory, 6 feet in height, she held in her hand; and this mechanical use of the shield may have involved contrivances of a complicated nature. Usually in restorations the serpent is represented as crouching within the shield, but this is directly contradicted by Pausanias, who says the serpent was near the spear, and therefore necessarily on the side opposite to the shield. Had he been curled up inside he would have hidden the sculpture of the shield almost entirely. Besides these objects, Pliny⁴ mentions a brazen sphinx, which was the most admired ornament of the pedestal; and has sometimes been confounded with the one that, according to Pausanias, adorned the helmet. That, however, was almost certainly of gold, with the whole helmet itself. The fact of this one being of brass, or rather of bronze, and its being mentioned in conjunction with the serpent and the spear, seems quite sufficient to show that they were grouped together about the base of the statue, and formed part of the general composition. Taking all the circumstances of the case into consideration, I see no escape from the restoration proposed by Quatremère de Quincy, with slight modification of course. Thus the statue stood grasping the spear in her right hand, and resting her left hand which supported the Victory on the rim of the shield, which was thus retained in an upright position.

One difficulty which Quatremère de Quincy did not meet is obviated in Plate IV.⁵ He represents Minerva as presenting the Victory to the Athenians, in which case doing so with her left hand would be awkward in the extreme. But if she is presenting the wreath to the goddess the case is different, and the figure may be held with equal propriety in either hand. That she did present the wreath to the goddess is probable from the Pergamon sculpture recently obtained from the Berlin museum, and nine-tenths of the representations on coins, &c.⁶ It must be confessed, however, that the numismatic evidence is in favour of the

¹ Jupiter Olympien, plate viii.
² Pliny, xxxvi. 5, p. 632.
³ Aristotle de Mundo; Valerius Max. s. 14, 6.
⁴ Periti mirantur et serpentem et sub ipsa cuspide aeream sphingem. Lib. xxxvi. ch. v.
⁵ In the section, Plate III., I have represented the goddess as restored by Quatremère de Quincy; but in the frontispiece, and in Plate IV., she is reproduced as on mature consideration I think she was most probably represented by Phidias.
⁶ The epithet "διαφανης" applied by Demosthenes (24. 121) to the wings of the Victory held in Minerva's hand seems to indicate that they were raised upward as shown in Plate IV., not hung downwards as they are represented in Plate III.

Victory being in the right hand, and generally she is represented as holding the spear in conjunction with the shield in her left. This is the theory adopted by the Duc de Luynes in his celebrated attempt to reproduce the chryselephantine statue in the original materials. If it is adopted, all the objects mentioned must be grouped on the left—the serpent near the spear, the sphinx "sub ipsa cuspide," and perhaps the owl.

There are, in fact, difficulties in the way of whichever theory we adopt, and it must rest eventually on a weighing of probabilities, for I fear there is no evidence by which the question can be settled definitely one way or the other.

The argument however in favour of the theory here adopted, which seems to me conclusive, is that if the statue was so arranged the light from the opaion falls directly on all those parts of the statue which were in ivory, and depended on light for their expression—the face, the arms, the Medusa's head, and the Victory, and to a less degree on the shield. The crest of the helmet, and the draperies, which were coloured, and could consequently express their own form independently of the mode in which the light was introduced, were left comparatively in the shade. So far as I am capable of forming an opinion the mode of lighting is perfect for a statue arranged as shown in the frontispiece, but would be totally out of harmony with any other form that has been suggested. Before leaving the subject I may mention that the model when completed was placed facing the east and west, as the temple was in the Acropolis. The consequence was that the southern light is found so completely to overpower the northern, that it seems to be the only one used for illumination; the northern light being only useful for softening the shadows and preventing them from being hard or abrupt.

Pausanias is our most trustworthy guide. He saw the statue when it was entire, and was so much in the habit of observing objects of that sort that he is not likely to have been mistaken. He has not been convicted of any error in any description in his works; and if we are to rely on what he says alone, there seems little doubt that she held the spear in her right hand. It is most improbable he would begin his account by stating that she had a spear¹ in her hand, as the most prominent feature in the group; and then after a considerable interval revert to the shield which he states lies (κεῖται) at her feet. If she held both in

---

¹ A curious question arises from an assertion of Ampelius (Liber Memoralis, 8, 10); in describing the temple he says, " Ipsa autem dea habet hastam de gramine," which it does not seem possible to translate otherwise than " a spear of bamboo" !

This from an unknown author might safely be treated with ridicule, but Cicero makes one of his principal accusations against Verres that " Ethamne gramineas hastas—in quibus neque manufactura quidquam neque pulcritudo erat alba, sed tantum magnitudo incredibilis de qua vel audire satis esset " (lib. iv. 56).

These spears were stolen from the Temple of Minerva at Syracuse, and the description will not answer for any manufactured article or any reed but a bamboo, which may at that time have been rare and consequently considered valuable.

her left hand it is almost impossible that they should not be mentioned together as parts of the same group.¹

Another article in the permanent furniture of the temple, which was too important to be overlooked, was the peplos, which was almost undoubtedly suspended as a canopy over the head of the statue. Usually, of course, it is understood that the word peplos signifies a garment—a shawl—to be worn on the person, and this may be its meaning when applied to the peplos of Juno.² She might have worn hers as a shawl, but this does not seem to have been the case of the peplos of Minerva, which, from what we know of it, must have been singularly inappropriate for the purpose. It would, indeed, have hid the ægis and all the golden ornaments of her dress, which were the principal and most expensive parts of her costume as designed by Phidias. The amount of gold so applied, we are told, amounted to 40 talents,³ upwards of 100,000*l.*, and it is hardly likely that it should be covered up with a shawl. Fortunately we are now relieved from the theory that it was used as a curtain to shield the statue of the goddess, either from the weather, or, as it has been sometimes suggested, from the dust. With the exception of the statue itself, it was the most important ornament of the temple. It was every three years on the Panathenaic festival paraded through the city, as the sail of a ship, and brought to the Acropolis with a pomp and ceremony that was not accorded to any other object in any other temple we know of. To assume, therefore, that it was a mere weather screen, or article of utilitarian use, seems most untenable. What it resembled most was apparently the parapetasma, which in some temples was hung from the roof, in others raised up from the floor.⁴ These were as rich as colour and embroidery could make them, and were an article of temple furniture, meant probably to screen the image of the deity from the gaze of the ordinary frequenters of the temple when no service or form of worship was being performed. We know that there were parapetasmata in the great temples at Olympia and at Ephesus,⁵ and there may have been in other temples, but there certainly was none in the Parthenon, or it must have been mentioned somewhere. The inference seems to be that the peplos supplied its place, and was as rich in embroidery as they were—the only essential difference being that while the parapetasmata were hung vertically, the peplos was suspended horizontally over the head of the goddess as a canopy. Be this, however, as it

---

¹ Falkener in the frontispiece to his Dædalus reproduces Pausanias's description more literally than has been done by any one. He places the spear in her left hand, where by the way it looks singularly awkward. The Victory is in her right and the shield lies literally at her feet. This, however, seems quite inadmissible, as one of the principal features of the whole design was the engraving of the wars of the gods and giants and of the Lapithæ with which it was adorned. According to this arrangement neither side could be properly seen, and the inside—the more important—not seen at all.

² Pausanias, v. 16.
³ Thucydides, ii. 13.
⁴ Pausanias, lib. v. ch. xii. p. 105.
⁵ Loc. cit.

may, we know from a passage in Pollux[1] that the word had two distinct meanings, and could be interpreted as applying to a canopy or awning, and such from the context seems certainly to have been its meaning here. There is also a celebrated passage in the Ion of Euripides, quoted by Stuart,[2] and others, which seems to apply especially to this peplos of Minerva, and does so with such exactness that it has been considered as literally describing it as he had seen it suspended in the temple, and practically as used in the same manner. The one question for us here is, what was its extent? I have represented it in the drawing as of about 15 feet by 20 feet, and adorned by the representation of the heavenly host as described in the well-known passage of Euripides, describing that at Delphi, which is generally supposed, however, to apply to that of the Minerva of the Parthenon.

The scale of the drawing is too small to make all this clear, but from it the general scheme can probably be made out. In the four angles are the chariots bearing the sun, and opposite that night or the moon, between them those of Hesperus and Aurora. These are represented as coming through the signs of the Zodiac, within which the planets are represented as they were portrayed in antiquity. On a larger scale, and with more time, it is evident there are in this all the elements required for being elaborated into an object of great beauty, but this need not be attempted here. All that is necessary in the present instance is to indicate the class of objects to which the pepli belonged, and to show how unfitted they were for a garment, but how admirably well suited to form a canopy over a goddess, or as an object to be borne like the sail of a ship in the Panathenaic procession.

It is much to be feared that any one who has not devoted considerable time to the study of Greek art, and has not imbued himself with its principles and per-

---

[1] J. Pollux, vii. 13, Πέπλος ἔσθημα καὶ τὰ ὅμοια. Πέπλον δ' ἐστι ἄπλοῦν τὴν χρείαν ἐκ ὑφάναι τε καὶ ἐπιβάλλεσθαι καὶ ὅτι ἐπίβλημά ἐστι τεκμήριον ἂν τις ἐκ τοῦ τῆς Ἀθηνᾶς πέπλου.

[2] Stuart, vol. ii, p. 8.

Instant at his behest the pious youth
Uprears the enclosure of the ample tent,
Framed to exclude the sun's meridian blaze
Or the mild splendour of his parting ray.
Ranged in right lines the numerous stakes extend,
In length a hundred feet, in breadth a hundred.
Then from the treasury of the god he takes
The consecrated tapestry, splendid woof,
To clothe with grateful shade the wondrous scene.
First o'er the roof he spreads the skirted Peplus
(The skirts on every side hang waving down).
* * * * *
On the rich produce of the loom are wrought
The heaven within whose spacious azure round
The numerous host of stars collective shine.
His coursers there, down to his western goal
The sun has driven. His last expiring beams
Draw forth the radiant light of Hesperus.
In sable stole night urges on amain,
With slackened reins, her steeds and dusky car.
The constellations on their swarthy queen
Attend; then through mid heaven win their way
The Pleiades, his sword Orion grasps,
Above them shines the Bear. * * *
* * * And glowing in the east Aurora,
The harbinger of day, that from the sky
Chases night's glittering train.
Ion, act iv. scene 1.

fections, will hardly realize from the outline drawings and diagrams of this work the beauties of the interior of the Parthenon. No drawing, indeed, can well convey a correct impression of such an interior, even to the practised eyes of an architect, and without colour, the effect even then is cold and misleading. Something might be done to represent its beauties by the construction of a model, about twice the size of that I have made, and painting it in accordance with what we know of the colour of the original. With a cella five feet in length, and an image of the goddess two feet in height, something might be done to reproduce the effect of the interior. But who is to do it? In Paris or at Berlin artists might be found who, under proper superintendence, could execute such a work, but hardly in this country. All the present race of architects are so enamoured with the crudeness of gothic colouring or the vulgarities of the so-called Queen Anne style, that the purity of Greek art is abhorrent to their ideas. Owen Jones, had he been now alive, might have attempted it, and Cockerell, with his elegance and taste, would certainly have saved it from being vulgar; but though an exquisite draftsman he was no colourist, and could scarcely himself have attempted it. Hittorff might, and most probably would with success. But all these have passed away, together with the school of art they loved, and did so much to adorn.

Even if gilding alone were applied to those parts which were certainly in metal, irrespective of colour, it would go far to relieve the naked coldness of the interior. The aegis and helmet of the goddess were certainly of gold, and so also was the shield, and probably some parts of her dress were relieved by golden fringes and bullion. The bronze grilles in the windows and the balustrades were certainly gilt, and the bronze ornaments of the roof were also, without doubt, heightened by gilding to a considerable extent.

If this gilding were applied it might do something to redeem the poverty-stricken look of a model, but it would go a very little way towards enabling any one to realize the effect of the cella of the Parthenon in its original state. The walls were certainly painted, probably in deep Venetian red or maroon colour, with a dark dado, and relieved by frets and ornaments of the infinity of patterns the Greeks knew so well how to design. The main roof of the building was probably in cedar displaying its natural colours, but the roofs of the galleries would certainly be adorned with patterns like those found by Mr. Penrose[1] on the roofs of the Propylæa close at hand. The abacus of the columns we know was adorned with a fret, and the echinus was probably ornamented with one of the numerous varieties of the honeysuckle pattern—probably all differing—of which the Greeks were so fond.

There is, in fact, no reason for doubting that the interior of the Parthenon was as richly and as completely adorned with colour as our most ornate drawing-

[1] Penrose, Principles of Athenian Art, pls. 22 and 26.

rooms or festal halls, and, carried out with all the skill and taste that characterized the age of Pericles, it probably surpassed in beauty anything seen before or since.

But in addition to these permanent decorations both the Parthenon and the Hekatompedon were crowded to an almost inconceivable extent by the offerings of the votaries of the goddess. Crowns of gold and wreaths of every form, curtains and tissues, of every conceivable variety, statues and statuettes, and jewellery, and objets d'art of every sort, testified to the devotion of the worshippers, and the wealth that was devoted to its expression.[1] No mediæval shrine of the most fashionable saint of the Christian church had ever such a wealth of votive offering presented to it as the Parthenon had, and none, we may safely add, that could be compared with it for beauty of design or faultlessness of execution.

In the preceding pages very little has been said with regard to the exterior of the Parthenon. Its forms and details have been so thoroughly investigated by Mr. Penrose,[2] and its proportions by him and Mr. Watkiss Lloyd, that nothing I could say would add any value to their investigations. Neither of them, however, attempts to explain how the colour was applied to the exterior, nor indeed has any one else except in the most perfunctory way. He would, indeed, be a bold man who would attempt it, and a very skilful one who would succeed in reproducing anything like the original scheme of decoration. With the interior the case is different. There the parts are so small and so various in their form that they seem to challenge colour to reduce them to harmony, and they lend themselves to it in every way. There is, on the other hand, a noble simplicity about the exterior, and a frequent repetition of the same parts, that looks as if the white marble were intended to tell its own tale, and as if colour would only serve to accentuate the inherent monotony of the architecture. Yet there is no doubt that colour was applied to the exterior, though perhaps not to the same extent as to the interior. The shafts of the columns were probably left plain, and only the echinus and the abacus adorned with colour. The architrave was probably left without colour, and only adorned with shields, and possibly with wreaths in metal in some parts. The metopes, however, were certainly painted, the figures probably imitating nature, with a background of blue, which also was most probably the colour of the triglyphs. The upper moulding of the cornice was rich as colour could make it, and traces of it are still to be detected on the marble,[3] and there are numerous examples of coloured cymatia in Sicily

---

[1] A list of these votive offerings to the shrine will be found in Michaelis' Parthenon, pp. 285 and 297.

[2] True Principles of Athenian Architecture. See Mr. Watkiss Lloyd's views, &c.; Appendix to Mr. Cockerell's Ægina and Bassæ; and a separate pamphlet published by John Weale in 1863.

[3] Penrose, Athenian Architecture, pl. i.

which render the restoration of these parts easy and certain.[1] The pediments were, of course, treated in the same manner as the metopes.

It is difficult to feel certain how the external walls of the cella were treated. There seems little doubt but they were painted of a rich warm colour—red?—but whether they were adorned with figure subjects interspersed throughout their whole height, or whether they were only adorned with panelling and other architectural designs, is still uncertain. My own impression is in favour of the former hypothesis, though it must be confessed if this were so, it seems strange that neither Pausanias, nor any one, should have mentioned them. The adornment of the Parthenon must have engaged the best art that the age of Pericles could command, and they would surely be worthy of notice from those who visited that famous temple.

However these questions may be settled eventually, we may rest assured that all the Greeks knew of polychromatic art was lavished on the decoration of the Parthenon. We know enough both of its architecture and of its sculpture, from what remains of them, to feel certain that no building formed with human hands ever reached the same degree of technic and æsthetic perfection as it did, and we cannot doubt that its painting at least equalled the sister arts. Colour was indispensable to reduce the whole to harmony, and we cannot conceive the Greeks employing it except in such a manner as would heighten the effect of the whole. We have few material proofs of the perfection they attained in this art, but they themselves had no hesitation in considering the degree of perfection they attained in colour as equal to that they had reached in either building or sculpture, and to their judgment we must defer. Combined as the three arts were together in the Parthenon, they produced what we must consider as the most perfect building the world has yet seen, and the one consequently most worthy of our most earnest study and contemplation.

— — —

This work has extended beyond the limits I proposed when it was undertaken. It may to many appear to have been a very simple process to describe the Parthenon and the mode in which it was lighted, and that all that was requisite might be said in much less space than is here employed. So many collateral issues have, however, arisen in the course of the investigation, that could not be passed over in silence, that the subject has, it seems, inevitably grown to its present dimensions. Without entering on many points of the primitive construction of Greek temples, it seemed almost impossible to make many features of the Parthenon intelligible; and without tracing the forms

---

[1] Hittorff, Architecture Antique de la Sicile, pls. 45 and 56. Coloured Cymatia were also found in the excavations at Olympia. Adolf Bœtticher, Olympia, pl. v.

of the metopes through a long series of examples it seemed hopeless to attempt to make it apparent how they were developed into the clerestory of that most beautiful of Greek temples.

Without attempting to explain how light was introduced into Roman temples also would have been to leave the subject pretty much as I found it. They form more than half of the number that have reached our times, and any attempt to apply the Greek mode of lighting to their remains would have made the confusion previously existing worse confounded. In order to arrive at any satisfactory conclusion on the subject, it seemed necessary to look at the templar arrangements of the ancients as a whole, and to omit nothing that could tend to elucidate the matter in hand. Hence perhaps what may in some instances appear unnecessary prolixity, but on the whole it seemed difficult to avoid it, at least to the extent in which this work is open to that charge. In order to state the case fully, I have attempted to meet every difficulty as it occurred, and I am not aware of any question that has been shirked or slurred over. Others must judge how far the explanations have been always satisfactory, but so far as I can form an opinion, the evidence is conclusive on nearly every point of the controversy. In so far as circumstantial evidence is concerned—if the expression may be used in such a connexion—I do not think a more complete case could well be made out; but, on the other hand, if direct material evidence is demanded, I fear it is not likely to be obtained—unless, indeed, some new discovery brings to light some templar forms now unknown. At present we must believe that the roofs of all the Greek temples were framed in wood, and have consequently rotted and decayed; and of the Roman temples—except that at Nîmes—not one is known to retain its original vault, and it is hardly sufficient to prove the case, though it is a satisfactory addition to the other evidence.

On one other point we might reasonably expect to procure direct material evidence, and its not being attainable may seem to weigh against the argument above stated. If the drainage of the opaion was in all—or most—instances to the peristyle, we might expect to find some marks of lions' heads remaining, or some pipes through the cella walls indicative of the existence of such an arrangement. So far as I know, however, no cella wall exists so complete as to afford evidence either for or against this view. At one time I thought the Theseion would be sufficient, but the upper courses of its walls have been so altered to admit of the vault the Christians threw over it, that they are of no avail. The cella walls of the Parthenon, and the temples at Pæstum, and all other Greek temples known, have disappeared, as indeed it is most likely they would in early times. They were built up of small squared stones, admirably adapted to utilitarian purposes, and consequently utilized as a quarry as soon as the temples were desecrated.

To my mind these and any other minor difficulties that may still appear to beset the argument seem to be of very small importance when weighed against the great principle which appears to me to pervade the whole controversy. It seems absolutely indispensable that any proposal that shall be made should provide a roof to the temples that should be constructively perfect, in a mechanical sense, and should admit the light in a manner which artistically should be as nearly perfect as we can conceive it to be. No theory, it appears to me, is worthy of a moment's consideration which does not show a mode of roofing Greek and Roman temples which was as perfectly water-tight as a roof could be before the introduction of window glass, and at the same time provided for the admission of the necessary amount of daylight, in as artistic a manner as we at all events can conceive. Their architects certainly surpassed any that have since succeeded in imparting a degree of artistic and monumental perfection to their temples that have never been surpassed, and it seems like treason to suppose they could not conquer the small mechanical difficulties involved in their construction.

INDEX.

Abacus, the, occasionally used in Egypt, 65.
Achaia, tile from, in British Museum, still retaining its paint, 79.
Ægina, temple of, of value as retaining nearly complete its original arrangements, 8 and 72.
Agrigentum, the temple at, one of the largest, but, at the same time, the least artistic temple erected by the Greeks, 91; interior of, divided into three parts by longitudinal walls, making two aisles, each 37 feet wide, 92.
Apollo Epicurius, detailed account of the temple of, at Bassæ, 74; the arrangements of the interior as sacrificed to the symmetry of the exterior, 76; external and internal columns probably of the same heights or nearly, 79.
Apollo Epicurius, statue of, not placed in the cella of his temple, as was the usual custom, 80.
Arch, the, before the time of the Etruscans, an architectural feature of the Egyptians, and a favourite mode of construction with the Etruscans, as in the case of the Cloaca Maxima, 24.
Assos, temple of, value of the recent researches at, of Mr. Clarke and the American archæologists, 89–90; judgment of Mr. Clarke that it cannot be earlier than B.C. 475, the date of the battle of Mycale, ib.; probably had internal pillars or pilasters to support an opaion, or some contrivance for lighting the cella, ib.; the sculptures from, now and long since in the Louvre, ib.
Athenian architecture, effect of its introduction into England in the last half of the xviiith century, 103.

Baalbec, architectural value of the Temple of Jupiter at, 12.
Basilica, the Regal, the form of buildings copied by the early Christians for their churches, 27.

Beni Hassan, tombs at, show segmental roof which could only have been suggested by arch construction, 24; Proto-Doric, as used in, the exact complement of the Greco-Doric order, 65.
Boetticher, C., reply by, to Dr. L. Ross, with quotations from Justinian's Digests, 4; character of the restoration by, of the Temple of Neptune at Pæstum, 5; suggestion by, that there was a window on each side the door of the Erechtheum, 101.
Bronze, of early use, especially in the Treasuries of Mycenæ and Orchomenos, 114.
Buleuterion at Cyzicus, roof so constructed as to be removable at will, 61.

Canina, M., scheme proposed by, in 1844 for lighting the Parthenon superior to any previously suggested, 4.
Ceilings, flat, in wood or plaster, unknown in classical times, 114.
Chaitya caves, all those executed before the Christian era literal copies of wooden buildings, 27.
Chipiez, M., article by, in the 'Revue Archéologique' for April 1878, in which he mainly adopts the second suggestion of M. Hittorff for lighting Greek temples, 7.
Christians, the early, rarely adopted for their churches Pagan temples, 21; made few changes in the internal arrangements of the classical temples or Basilicas, 115, note—ep. Church of Sta. Agnese in Rome.
Cockerell, Prof., great value, artistically, of his work on the 'Temples of Ægina and Bassæ,' 8–9; Ionic columns in his "Taylor Institute" at Oxford, copied from those found by him at Bassæ, but used only as ornaments, 9.
Coins, of Hadrian, Antoninus Pius, and Diadumenianus, showing the semicircular vault of Hadrian's temple at Jerusalem, 25.
Corinth, temple at, not earlier than B.C. 650, 65.

Cyrene, rock-cut temple at, of great value and interest as a model, 45.

Daphne, temple of, perhaps the model of that of Jupiter Olympius, built by Cossutius, 20; the second great hypæthral one, ib.

Donaldson, Prof., gives a view of coin, showing the circular roof of the great temple at Samos, 22.

Doric architecture employed for secular buildings down to Imperial Roman times, 52; object of, to provide for the gods nobler abodes than the dwellings of men, 56.

Doric pillars, the, a copy from an Egyptian original, such as in a tomb at Beni Hassan, 64 and 65.

Dörpfeld, Prof., notice of paper by, in 'Oeffentlicher Anzeiger,' 11; suggesting his finding at Olympia the "hypæthron" and "impluvium" of the temple, 11; diagram of roof of the arsenal of Philon, 95, note.

Egypt, generally admitted that there existed in it a Proto-Doric style, 53; the only country that could have contributed anything towards the development of the Grecian style of architecture, ib.; the rainless climate of, allowed of the employment of flat roofs, 100.

Eleusis, propylæa of temple at, a copy of an ancient amphiprostyle one, 66; first examined by the explorers of the Dilettanti Society in 1797, and more fully in 1817, 96; archaeologically of great interest, ib.; description of, by Plutarch, in his life of Pericles, 97; special interest in, from the connection between the worship of Ceres and that of the Egyptian Isis, 97–8; almost exactly one half of the size of the hall at Karnak, 99; almost certainly copied from an Egyptian design, ib.

Elis, temple of, Pausanias's date for, B.C. 570, 84; according to the German explorers commenced about B.C. 460, and finished in B.C. 457, ib.; dimensions of, slightly greater than those of Pæstum, ib.; the architecture of, very inferior in style, &c., 86.

Ephesus, the Temple of Diana at, the third of the great Asiatic hypæthrals, 32; as the western front faced the city and the port, all the skill of the architects was lavished upon this, 33; diagram showing the arrangement of the 127 columns round, &c., 34; nothing like the "columnæ cælatæ" of, found anywhere else in ancient architecture, 35; strong probability that the frieze of, was in bronze, 36; insufficient evidence of opisthodomos as suggested by Mr. Wood, 37.

Ephesus, temple of, the cella of, probably a great hall, 70 feet wide by 150 feet in length, 37.

Erechtheum, three windows in the W. wall of, 101–2.

Falkener, Mr. Ed., error of, in supposing that Pliny's 26 cubits applies only to the statue of Minerva, 3; in his 'Dædalus' proposes a semicircular roof for the Parthenon, &c; answer by, to what he conceived to be unjust criticism on his 'Dædalus,' 10.

Fergusson, J., general views of, on the subject of the "hypæthron," in his 'True Principles of Beauty in Art,' 10; paper by, at the Royal Institute of British Architects, in November, 1861, 11.

François Vase, illustrations of early temple-architecture from, 58.

Garnier, M., restoration by, of the so-called Temple of Jupiter at Ægina, published in 'Revue Archéologique,' 1854, 61; value of his researches in the temple of Ægina, 73, note.

Gordian, coin of, valuable as showing the semicircular roof of the temple at Miletus, 22.

Greek architecture, the primæval wooden, generally to be recognized in the subsequent stone, 57.

Greek peristylar temples, general character of, 68; probably of Egyptian origin, 69; may date as early as B.C. 700, ib.; the earliest examples of, at Ortygia in Sicily, and Metapontum in Magna Græcia, ib.

Greek temples, no one of them of any importance built later than B.C. 325 (the age of Alexander the Great), 15; the earliest (before B.C. 700) unquestionably of wood, 52; the original idea of, a square or oblong hall to contain the image, with a porch to protect the doorway, 58; when properly studied show great variety of design, especially in their interiors, 67; none of the features of the external decoration of, go through to the inside, 70; the cellas of, generally columnar, 71; alteration and modification of, when converted into Christian churches, 89; no passage in ancient authors stating how they were roofed, 111; stairs of, generally inserted in the thickness of the eastern wall, as at Pæstum and Agrigentum, 116.

INDEX.

Greeks, the, able to put a weather-tight roof on their buildings and at the same time to provide sufficient light for their interiors, 9; indeed, the most ingenious and artistic people ever yet known, 15.

Hadrian, temple of, at Jerusalem, destroyed about the time of Constantine, 25; completes the Temple of Jupiter Olympius at Athens, and builds that of Venus and Roma at Rome, 47.
Heraion, at Olympia, wholly unknown till recently excavated by the Germans, 86; in many ways peculiar, with greater relative proportions than those of any other temple in Greece Proper, ib.; really a sort of statue-gallery, 88; story in Pausanias of the Hoplite whose body was found on, ib.; a copy of the interior of, well fitted for a gallery of casts, ib., note; statement in Pausanias, that one of the original wooden columns had been preserved therein, probably as a curiosity, 89.
Hermes, statue of, by Praxiteles, found by the Germans *in situ*, 88.
Hittorff, in his 'Architecture Antique de la Sicile,' refutes Boetticher's views, 5, note; practically adopts the views urged by Mr. Fergusson twenty years earlier for his restoration of the great temple at Selinus, 7.

Ilyssus, the small temple at, lighted from the front, 66.
India, twenty to thirty cave-temples in, lighted in the way suggested for Greek temples, 24; no stone architecture in, before the reign of Asoka, B.C. 250, 26.
Indian temples, lighting of, probably derived from Greek originals, 26.

Jupiter Olympius, the temple of, first contemplated by Peisistratus, but not built, 17; owing to the energy of Mr. Penrose we now know exactly the height and form of the capitals of the pillars of the present structure, 18; of the interior we know nothing, owing to the obstructiveness of the Archaeological Society of Athens, ib.; Sylla removed some of the internal columns of, to adorn the Capitol at Rome, ib.; ultimately built, at the expense of Antiochus Epiphanes, by a Roman architect, Cossutius, ib.; three ranges of columns still existing in front of the *naos* at the east end, 19; not certain whether it faced the east or west, ib.; all certainly known of it, is that it was decastyle and dipteral, 20; not conceivable that it could have been entirely roofless, as stated by Vitruvius, ib.; probably lighted by a great eastern or western window, 21.

Karli, Chaitya temple of, about the same date as that of Jupiter Olympius, 25.
Karnac, temple of, the mode of lighting adopted in, that subsequently imitated by the Greeks, 54; perfection, as a structure, of the Great Hall at, 99; the most massive and most sublime of all architectural creations, 105.

Labrouste, M., description by, of the temple at Paestum, published by the 'Ecole des Beaux Arts,' 1877, and its character, 5.
Letronne and Raoul Rochette (in France), advocate, generally, the same views as Ross and Boetticher, 5.
Lorenzo, San, fuori le Mura, value of, as showing how the Pagan gradually faded into the Christian styles, 114, note.
Louvre, statue just placed in, probably the most archaic known, 30, note.
Luynes, Duc de, attempt to reproduce Phidias's chryselephantine statue of Minerva, 121.

Mammeisi, the name of certain quasi peripteral temples found in Egypt, 69.
Metopes, progressive changes in, 70.
Minerva, shield of, elaborately carved on both sides, 121; so placed as to support the arm of the statue, and the Victory, 6 feet high, the Goddess held in her hand, 121.
Moussmieh, so-called prætorium at, has many resemblances, quâ lighting, to the Temple of Diana at Nimes, 40.
Mosta in Malta, remarkable alterations in the church at, 95.
Myron, the treasury of, at Olympia, noticed by Pausanias, but not yet discovered by the Germans, 55.

Nike Apteros, small temple of, lighted through the front wall, 66.
Nimes, the "Maison Carrée" at, and the Temple of Jupiter in the Forum at Pompeii, most likely lighted from their doors only, 48; the only one that retains its vault in its entirety, 39; North, Miss, gallery in Kew Gardens, prepared for, lighted as the Parthenon by its opaion, 109, note.

154   INDEX.

Olia, temple of, suggested ridge piece at, 57, note.
Olive-tree, the Sacred, shown by Messrs. Michaelis and Fergusson to have been planted in the open air of the Pandrosium, 102.
Olympia, Temple of Jupiter at, the entire ground-plan recently disclosed by the German excavations, 84.
Omar, Mosque of, at Jerusalem, probably in part built from the ruins of Hadrian's temple, 23.
Opaion, the name given to an internal metope or clerestory-opening, 73-4; is, in fact, the true principle by which all Greek temples were lighted, 97.
Ortygia, the temple at, the oldest example of the completed Doric order, 74.

Pæstum, Temple of Neptune at, contains, *in situ*, more of the internal arrangements than any other Doric temple which exists, 84; drawings made by Mr. Wilkins, probably very accurate, 85; no doubt about its plan, or as to the external order of its pillars, *ib.*; floor of the cella at, 6 feet above that of the peristyle, 84; almost an exact counterpart of the recently excavated Temple of Jupiter at Olympia, *ib.*; Herodotus's date for B.C. 543, *ib.*
Pantheon, the, at Rome, not originally erected for a temple, but as the Laconicum of the Baths of Agrippa, 49; very like in its arrangements to that of the Baths of Caracalla, *ib.*; statues of the gods in, arranged in niches round the walls as in a serapeum, 50; no evidence that any other temple besides it was lighted by a hole in the roof, 51.
Parthenon, model of, as constructed by Mr. Fergusson, value of as showing how this building must have been lighted, 12; the actual temple, so placed that its roof could not be seen, except from distant hills, 76; the most perfect specimen of architectural art as yet erected anywhere, 103; nearly perfect up to the explosion of 1687, 104; character of the changes made to fit it for a Christian church, 106; converted into a Christian church probably between the age of Constantine and Justinian, *ib.*; visit to and description by Messrs. Spon and Wheeler in 1676, 106; domes placed on the roof of, before the time of Justinian, 106-7; interior of, divided into two principal apartments, the opisthodomos and the hekatompedon, 109; clerestory of, probability that columns of the Corinthian order were then used, 109; Boetticher discovered two doorways leading from the opisthodomos to the hekatompedon, 110; the timbers in the roof of, an important feature in its decoration, 112; diagram showing the plan and elevation of the opening of its roof, 118; the suggested construction of the roof of, provides ample light for the statue of Minerva, 120; the walls of the cella of, originally painted, probably in maroon or Venetian red, 125; arrangement for the peplos impossible if its roof was flat, 113; stairs in, originally of wood, long since disappeared, 116; description by Pausanias of the statue of Minerva in, 120; question as to how the shield of Minerva was placed, 120-121; the restoration proposed by M. Quatremère de Quincy, on the whole the best, 121; value of the evidence of Pausanias about the statue of Minerva in, as he saw this while intact, 122; the peplos probably suspended as a canopy over the head of the goddess, 123; traces of colour found on the upper moulding of the cornice of, 126; remarkable wealth of, in votive offerings, *ib.*; some colour doubtless applied to the exterior, but only partially, *ib.*
Pelasgi, artistic style of, apparently disappeared on the return of the Heraclidæ, but their metallic skill was preserved, 54; artistic period of, probably as early as B.C. 1880, 54.
Penrose, Mr., work by, on the 'Principles of Athenian Architecture,' first clearly showed the Parthenon's wonderful superiority to anything else, 104.
Peplos, the, probably spread horizontally over the goddess's head as a canopy, 123; adorned with a representation of the heavenly host, 124.
Phidias, chryselephantine statue by; difficulty as to the space for it in the temple of Elis, 85.
Philon, roof of arsenal at, as reconstructed by M. Dörpfeld, 64, note and diagram.
Pliny, assertion by, that the temple of Ephesus had 127 columns, cannot be disregarded, 33.
Pseudo-hypæthral temples, description of, 59-54.

Quincy, Q. de, 'Essai sur le Jupiter Olympien,' 1815, 1; quotes and refutes the views of Spon and Wheeler, Perrault, Gagliani, Simon, Barthélemy, and others, *ib.*; adopts his form of roof chiefly from a passage in Strabo, 2; discusses the views of Mr. Stuart very fully,

INDEX. 135

in an essay published in 1826, ib.; the first to support the idea of lighting the temples by partially removing their roofs, ib.; the views of, adopted by Edward Falkener, 3; supported in his view by the fact that there are many coins representing the interior of temples with arched forms over the statues, ib.; restoration of the statue of Minerva by, literally follows Pausanias, 124.

Rhamnus, the temple at, pre-Hellenic, 65.
Rhamses II., temple of, at Abydos, offers a striking examples of arch-construction, 24.
Roman temples, no one built earlier than B.C. 75, unless that of Jupiter Olympius at Athens be included in this category, 15.
Roofs, mode whereby the primitive ones were formed by the Greeks, 61; open timber, common at all times, and especially in the Middle Ages, 113.
Ross, Dr. Ludwig, views of, in his 'Der Hypæthral-Tempel,' 4.

Samos, the great temple of, built by Rhoecus, the son of Philens, 28; many and remarkable differences from other temples at, 29; possible suggestion that its style was not Ionic, ib.
Saws, the invention of, ascribed by the Greeks to Dædalus, 60.
Schliemann, M., architectural value of his discoveries at Mycenæ and Orchomenos, 54; gold work found by, at Mycenæ, &c., contemporary with the structures in which they were discovered, 55; the people whose tombs, &c., he excavated may have had affinities with the Egyptians, but this did not in any way influence Doric architecture, ib.; important to note that in his researches, no evidence was met with that letters were known or ever used, ib.; excavations of, also, show that the builders of the places he dug up had many affinities with the Phrygians and Etruscans, ib.
Selinus, Great Temple of, the various plans for its restoration unsatisfactory, whether proposed by Messrs. Hittorff and Zanth, or by the Duca di Serra di Falco, 94; not finished when shaken down by an earthquake, 96.
Sminthian Apollo, Temple of the, ornament in imitation of bronze, from a capital of, 115.
Staircases in stone still observable on each side of the entrance of the great temple at Baalbec, 44.

"Stratura," the meaning of, in Justinian's Digests, 4; no evidence that this plan, adopted for private houses A.D. 500, was used by the Greeks for their temples B.C. 500, ib.

Tegea, temple at, considered by Pausanias to be superior to that of Apollo Epicurius, 80; arrangements of, similar to those of Basse, 84.
Temples, circular, the mode of lighting, 49.
Temples, Greek, dates of, none before B.C. 700, or after B.C. 300, 52.
Temples, the lighting of, as planned by the Greeks, not carried out by the Roman architects, 14.
Temples, Roman, lighted by a modification of the hypæthral arrangement of certain Greek temples, 14; but there does not seem to have been any particular system, 50.
Triglyph, the, the most peculiar and marked constructive feature in the composition of the Parthenon, 59; original conception of, and mode of forming, 60.
Troy, Siege of, the warriors at, connected with the Phrygians and Pelasgi, and not necessarily acquainted with what we call Classical Greeks, 55, note.

Ulricus, M., a learned man and good draughtsman, but no architect, 57, note.

Venus and Rome, Hadrian's Temple of, the largest and most beautiful temple in Rome, 45.
Vitruvius, little value of the testimony of, on the question of lighting temples, 15; the text of, avowedly tampered with, ib.; reflections on the passage in his work referring to the "lighting" of temples, 16–17; the Temple of Jupiter Olympius at Athens, described by, the only one decastyle and dipteral existing in Europe, ib.; real meaning of his words, "medio sub divo et sine tecto," 21; when he wrote Grecian-Doric was well-nigh forgotten, 53; never alludes to the temples of Pæstum or Sicily, though these must have been familiar to many Romans, ib.

Walhalla, built by Klenze, as a facsimile of the Parthenon, but with many defects of detail, 107, note.
Wood, Mr., value of his researches at Ephesus, 52.
Wren, Sir Christopher, and his contemporaries recognized no essential difference between the early mediæval churches and those of Queen Anne's times, 14.

LONDON
PRINTED BY WILLIAM CLOWES AND SONS, LIMITED,
STAMFORD STREET AND CHARING CROSS.

TEMPLE OF JUPITER OLYMPIUS AT ATHENS.

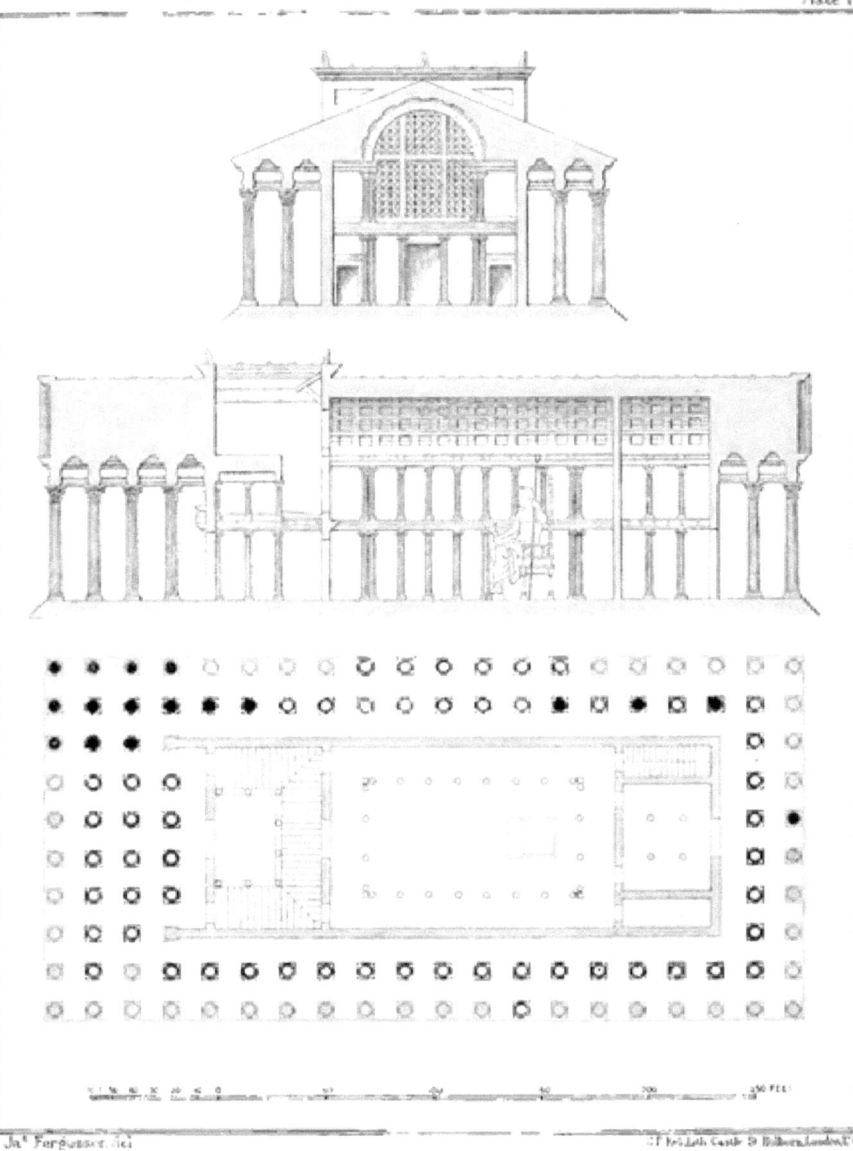

TEMPLE OF APOLLO EPICURIUS. BASSÆ.

Transverse Section.

Exterior. Interior.
Plan of Roof.

External Elevation.

Internal Elevation.

SECTION OF THE CELLA OF THE PARTHENON.

VIEW OF THE INTERIOR OF THE CELLA OF THE PARTHENON

www.ingramcontent.com/pod-product-compliance
Lightning Source LLC
Chambersburg PA
CBHW030342170426
43202CB00010B/1209